if you're

clueless

about

financial

planning

and

want to

know more

SETH GODIN

JOHN PARMELEE

 Dearborn
Financial Publishing, Inc.®

If You're Clueless about Financial Planning and Want to Know More

This publication is designed to provide accurate and authoritative information in regard to the subject matter covered. It is sold with the understanding that the publisher is not engaged in the rendering of legal, accounting, or other professional service. If legal advice or other expert assistance is required, the services of a competent professional person should be sought.

Editorial Director: Cynthia A. Zigmund
Managing Editor: Jack Kiburz
Interior and Cover Design: Karen Engelmann

Published by Dearborn Financial Publishing, Inc.®

Printed in the United States of America
98 99 00 10 9 8 7 6 5 4 3 2 1

Library of Congress Cataloging-in-Publication Data
Godin, Seth.
    If you're clueless about financial planning and want to know more / Seth Godin, John Parmelee.
        p.   cm.
    Includes index.
    ISBN 0-7931-2988-5
    1. Finance, Personal. I. Parmelee, John. II. Title.
    HG179.G634   1998
    332.024–dc21
                                                            98-30390
                                                            CIP

Other Clueless books by Seth Godin:

If You're Clueless about Mutual Funds and Want to Know More

If You're Clueless about Retirement Planning and Want to Know More

If You're Clueless about Saving Money and Want to Know More

If You're Clueless about the Stock Market and Want to Know More

If You're Clueless about Insurance and Want to Know More

If You're Clueless about Starting Your Own Business and Want to Know More

If You're Clueless about Accounting and Finance and Want to Know More (with Paul Lim)

If You're Clueless about Getting a Great Job and Want to Know More (with Beth Burns)

If You're Clueless about Selling and Want to Know More

Acknowledgments

Thanks to Jack Kiburz and Cynthia Zigmund at Dearborn for their invaluable editorial guidance; Karen Watts, who created the Clueless concept; and Laura Spinale who pulled it all together.

Thanks, too, go to Linda Carbone and the rest of the crew at SGP for their never-ending insight and hard work.

Contents

GETTING
a clue
about
financial
PLANNING

This book is written for you if you're wondering if you're making the right choices about your money. Maybe you have a job that pays good money, a family, a car, and a home— the whole American dream.

Or maybe you're starting up a business of your own and trying to find the funds to make it successful while still providing for your family. Or maybe you're trying to pay off a mortgage while at the same time saving money to go back to school to boost your career. Or maybe you'd love to play the stock market but don't know where to get solid investment information.

What Are the Stakes?

No matter which scenario best fits your life there is one reality we all face: We have to be smart about the way we save and invest the money we make—because no one else is looking out for us. No one.

For example, when it comes time to retire, many Americans will not be guaranteed the same financial safety net that current retirees enjoy. Each generation will be affected differently. Twentysomethings will be hit the hardest, followed by the Baby Boomers. Either way, by the early part of the next century, Social Security, the federal retirement fund, will not exist in the way it does today; neither will Medicare, the national health care program for the elderly.

The U.S. Department of Health and Human Services projects that Medicare's hospital insurance fund will be insolvent in 2002. And government forecasters predict that the Social Security retirement fund will be empty by 2029. That's right, empty.

Both Congress and the president are currently searching for ways to reform these programs, either by cutting costs and/or increasing revenues. That may mean increasing the age of eligibility. That may mean some means-testing. That may mean decreasing benefits. Or it may mean some combination of the three. In any event it definitely means you'll have a greater financial responsibility to take care of yourself.

Why are we talking about issues like retirement when it might seem so far away? There are two easy reasons, and they make up the core of why you need to read this book. Reason number one: If you ever hope to achieve the kind of financial security needed for retirement, the time to start saving is now. You also need to start investing now, even if all you can contribute is $50 a month. That's okay. There are plenty of investment opportunities for that little a price.

Reason number two: You have to start thinking long-term. You're not a kid anymore.

Why You Need to Protect Your Money

You work hard. Maybe you know how to save what you make, and perhaps you're even learning how to invest it so that your nest egg grows and your retirement pic-

ture is shaping up. Be proud of yourself that you've started to build your financial future. But you can't stop now.

Just as there are forces of nature such as earthquakes and fire that threaten your personal security, there are life forces such as divorce, economic downturn, financial setbacks, lawsuits, and the IRS that threaten your well-being. And you need to be aware of these threats so you can take steps to safeguard yourself and your family.

Protection Advice

Asset protection is not just for the rich. You have more to shelter than you realize. In fact, you are likely part of one of the three economic groups that especially need to watch out for their personal finances: the financially comfortable upper middle class, the middle class, and those just struggling to pay their monthly bills. This book is not written for the rich, who can well afford an army of expensive tax attorneys, financial advisers, and other experts to help steer their money out of harm's way.

The good news for you is that today much of the saving and investing advice that used to be reserved for the wealthy can be accessed from a number of inexpensive sources: books, magazines, newspapers, even the Internet.

It's also important to remember that the best financial advice is simple, free, and hasn't changed in 50 years:

- Define what financial success means to you and then chart a course to meet those goals.

- Don't live someone else's definition of success.

- Start early (that means now!) with saving and investing your money and let the power of time and compounding work for you.

- Pay off your debts before the power of time and compounding works against you.

- Make saving and investing a habit.

- Accept that it's okay to get rich slowly.

- If an investment sounds too good to be true, keep your hands on your wallet and don't let go.

- Diversify.

- Stay within your risk tolerance.

- Don't put your money into anything you don't understand.

Who Needs to Protect Money?

If you're lucky enough to find yourself in the upper middle class, and you have assets like stock and bond investments, a house, and a car, you know you need to protect what you have and make your money grow for the future. If you're in the middle class, you know how easy it could be to lose what little assets you may have built up. You could lose your job, you could get sick.

Protecting what cash and other assets you have is also important for the middle class because taxes, both federal and state, tend to eat away more from the middle class's wallets than from the poor. The rich, too, can worry less since they can shelter their money from taxes in a variety of legal ways. If you have less disposable income to work with, you need to protect every dollar.

If you're part of the lower middle class, or the "working poor" as it has become fashionable to say, then protecting your money is a very serious matter. You may have few assets, but they may be more than you think. For example, if you have an entry-level job, now is the time to do a little exploring of the company to see what financial benefits it offers. Or if you're renting an apartment in a bad part of town, you might want to look into renter's insurance to protect what may be your only hard assets.

But no matter what group you belong to, there is one common obstacle: a lack of personal savings, which is your safety net if things go wrong in your life. Americans are among the worst savers in the industrialized world. The Japanese and the Germans, for example, currently save about 13 percent of their disposable income. In the

United States it's about 4 percent. Even worse, that number is decreasing. Twenty years ago Americans saved twice as much as today. The last time Americans saved this pitifully was during the Great Depression of the 1930s.

So it's up to you to save more and protect what you have. Remember, no one else will.

Profiles in Financial Courage

Now that you have a little of the bird's-eye view of what financial issues are out there, it's time for the worm's-eye view—the micro picture—because everyone has his or her own needs and desires, both personal and financial.

Morgan and JeNell Sibbald

Take Morgan and JeNell Sibbald, who have been married for four years. He's a senior research scientist at Goodyear in Akron, Ohio. She's a chemist like her husband, but she's currently between jobs as she looks for something that's up to her level. Their family income is around $50,000, they live in an apartment, and they have no real debts, except for some credit card bills.

Their future goals probably sound pretty familiar to you. "We would like to be in a house, we would like to purchase at least one new vehicle, possibly two, and we'd like to start a family," says Morgan. "Within five years we'd like to have at least one child, perhaps two. In that time I'd like to be building up some personal savings and investing, so I guess we're in a time of rapid change."

They know the importance of investing early for these long-term goals, but they just haven't gotten around to exploring all their financial options. "Time is the biggest factor in my life right now. It's hard enough for me to keep up with scientific journals," says Morgan, "much less read mutual fund prospectuses."

That's where this book can be of some help. For example, chapter 3 is designed for the inexperienced investor, as well as for investor wannabes. It discloses the risks and

rewards of investing, explains why stocks, bonds, and mutual funds belong in your personal financial plan, and shows how you can get started.

Luckily for the Sibbalds, Morgan works for a company that provides a fairly generous benefits package, including a standard defined-benefit pension plan and a 401(k). This type of defined-contribution plan allows Morgan to contribute up to 16 percent of his monthly salary (pretax), and the company matches that up to 6 percent. Morgan also has some control over how his nest egg is invested. "I split it up. I went 20 percent here and 30 percent there, and I went aggressive and moderate," he says. "I sought advice from somebody at work. I guess you could call him a mentor. I value his opinion, plus he drives a Lexus."

Deciding how to invest your retirement money can be maddening if you don't know what your options are and if you don't speak the lingo. Chapter 5 provides a detailed explanation of defined-benefit pensions, defined-contribution plans, Individual Retirement Accounts (IRAs), and the new Roth IRA.

Although many apartment renters choose not to insure their belongings, Morgan considers it a must. "It's about being in a building that many other people are living in and maybe someone knocks over a lamp, or whatever, and that could start a fire. I could lose everything, and it would be completely out of my control," he says. "I didn't want to be helpless."

So he took an inventory of all their possessions and went with that list to the same agent who handled his car insurance. That turned out to be a smart move since he was able to get a multipolicy discount. Now he pays just $100 a year for full replacement value coverage. Chapter 7 in this book looks at renter's insurance, what your coverage options are, and how you can save money on your premiums.

Jennifer Powell

Jennifer Powell is communications manager for the Delaware Economic Development Office. She has a good job paying around $40,000, and she also just bought a house, though recent car troubles have forced her to drive around in a beat-up 1983 Ford Fairmont loaner from her family. She's single, and the proud mother of two cal-

ico cats, named Amazing and Gracie. Her main financial needs right now are paying off her mortgage, paying down some credit card debt, and finding the money to pay for graduate school.

Like many people, Jennifer grew up in a house, and once she was on her own she never considered renting an apartment. Financial concerns dominated her decision to buy a home of her own. "I like the idea of building up equity and not throwing away my money every month. I'll get a sizable check back when I get my money back from taxes," she says. But there are also personal reasons why she puts up with the $800 monthly mortgage payments, which don't include bills for electricity, water, and sewer service. "I feel more at home than I would be in an apartment. It's my home, it's my yard, it's my apple tree," she says. "I've eaten an apple off of my apple tree and it's the best apple I've ever had."

To protect her home and possessions, Jennifer purchased homeowner's insurance. Since there are always financial risks in buying a home, it's important to find the right insurance plan for your needs. You can turn to chapter 7 in this book to explore your options.

The mortgage payments have taken a toll on her finances. And like many Americans, Jennifer has found that her credit card can often be her best friend (at least until the bill arrives). "While I was getting settled into the house that's what I used for basic expenses," she says. "Plus, before I bought the house I had a lot of fun traveling, and I used the credit card to pick up some neat stuff." Her excursions to Morocco and Israel, combined with other more basic purchases, account for credit card debt in excess of $5,000.

Although Jennifer has no problems staying financially afloat, many Americans (in fact, an all-time high number of Americans) can't make ends meet and file for bankruptcy. If you go to chapter 2 you'll find a discussion of how to reorganize your debts and tips on how to avoid getting yourself into that position in the first place.

Jennifer also wants to go back to school part-time to boost her career. She feels that a graduate degree in communications management will either lead to a promotion at her current job or be valuable elsewhere. The program's tuition is about $9,000 a year. Luckily for her, the Delaware Economic Development Office, like many

employers, has a tuition reimbursement policy, which may pick up part of her tuition if the classes are relevant to her job. Otherwise, she will have some family financial support. For more information on financing college, as well as deciding if it's worth it to go for extra education, just turn to chapter 4.

Like far too many Americans, Jennifer has no real investments, though she has about $6,000 socked away in an IRA. That's currently the only retirement plan she has; she won't be vested in her employer's pension plan until she's worked there for five years. But what if she doesn't stay there that long? "That's the thing," she says, "a lot of employees will be with the state for thirty years, but my kind of position is not the sort where I would be here for thirty years." To be successful, you must make retirement planning a priority decades before you're eligible for the gold watch. Chapter 5 examines the many investment options.

Like many employees who switch from job to job in search of career advancement, Jennifer has had to make use of federal laws that protect her employee benefits. A few years back she changed jobs from the New Castle County Chamber of Commerce to the Delaware Economic Development Office. When she jumped ship, she found that she also lost her health insurance coverage. Luckily, she knew about a federal law that goes by the acronym COBRA; chapter 6 examines this law in some detail.

"When I took this job it was on a casual seasonal basis, and I took it because it was too good to pass up. But what that meant was that I had to go on COBRA for a few months because seasonal employees don't get health insurance," Jennifer says. "However, once I was made a regular employee I could roll right into their coverage." She currently enjoys an employer-sponsored HMO plan.

While she loves her job, Jennifer says that outside factors can really ruin her day. "For a while I was getting these AOL messages that would have a Web site in them," she says. "I get messages all the time that are legitimate. With economic development we sometimes get investment requests, which we don't do, but you know, I'll get that kind of e-mail. But one time while I was getting one of these messages it was set up to go to a porn site. It got really annoying." Protecting your time, your privacy, and your money online is the topic of chapter 9.

Song Palmese and Family

Song and her husband, Michael Blank, live in Oakland, California, where they both have regular jobs and Song is also trying to make a go at starting up a small business. In addition Song's daughter, Summer, is just beginning kindergarten. Their personal finances are similar to those of many Americans who are married with children. "We are currently treading water. You know, we can breathe but we're not going anywhere," she says.

With work and family time pressures they simply don't have enough hours in the day to map out a financial plan and familiarize themselves with the many investment and tax issues that are out there. When asked if she knew about the so-called marriage bonus, Song laughed and said, "My marriage bonus is finding someone who will come home every night, you know. Someone who when Summer had chicken pox cheerfully took sick days from work so I could go to work because I make less money and I don't get paid sick time. I'd call that a marriage bonus." Actually the marriage bonus—and its counterpart, the marriage penalty—is a quirk in the tax law that might affect you and your spouse. For a closer look, just turn to chapter 2.

Song's start-up business, fittingly called SongBird Gifts (e-mail to: songbirdgifts@juno.com), hand-makes beaded bracelets, necklaces, and crocheted amulet bags. This side occupation provides some supplemental income, though eventually she wants to make SongBird her full-time profession. "I've always found that I'm happiest when I'm creating something," she says. "I don't do twelve hundred bracelets that are exactly the same. Everything that I do is at least slightly different. I find that I cannot repeat myself and I find that in beadwork I don't have to."

Although she started small, Song quickly found that getting the business off the ground was both time-consuming and costly. In its one year of existence, SongBird has had to deal with a lot of government red tape. "I needed to find out if I needed a city license as well as a state license. Did I need a license to sell as well as to make? Did I need to get a zoning change so that I could use my home address, which is an apartment, as a business address? If I were going to sell at craft fairs would I need a separate sales permit for each fair?" After many phone calls to local officials the answers came back—each attached to a price tag. Government regulations and fees included $30 for a city permit, $60 for city taxes, and $10 for zoning clearance to use her home address as a business address.

Song's run-in with government regulations was relatively tame, but it's important to realize how much of your paycheck goes to states and localities, and to Uncle Sam. Chapter 2 offers a broader picture of what you pay.

While Song can't count stocks and bonds among her assets, she clearly has an important investment. "I have one," she says, "and she's very wiggly." Summer represents a lot of joy, but she is also a financial concern that Song and Michael have had to take into account. They have not begun to save for college, but they have been able to scrape together the funds to pay for private schooling for her lower education. Summer's private kindergarten costs about $9,000, $5,000 of which is paid with assistance through the school, and the remaining $4,000 comes through family support. Chapter 4 can help you get started if you also have a young child who will some day have plenty of college bills to be paid.

Michael's job as a deputy court clerk in the San Mateo County court system provides around $30,000 in income, plus benefits like a defined-benefit pension plan and managed health care coverage. Those benefits are vital since Song's regular job as a secretary for a consulting firm is only part-time, with no pension or health plan, and pays out just $8,000 a year. Michael also has life insurance through his job, so the family has at least a basic safety net should there be an accident. Like many Americans, Song has no will, which doesn't concern her given that her assets are limited.

Knowing where and how to get insurance and retirement benefits is especially valuable if you have a family that depends on you. Chapter 6 examines managed care and other types of health coverage. Chapter 5 details what types of retirement options are available. And chapter 8 explains why it's important to have a will and why estate planning is something to look at even when you're still young and healthy.

Michael Gekas

Michael Gekas is a Virginia native who recently received a degree in business economics at the University of California at Santa Barbara. He's read the *Wall Street Journal* since he was 12, and he loves to play the stock market. His financial needs are quite different from Song's; he has no dependents, and subsequently he has much more of an ability to take financial risks.

Michael is heavy into stocks, with about 70 percent of his investments in equities and around 30 percent in bond mutual funds and cash. He thinks of himself as a so-called value investor. "That's my biggest thing," he says. "I like the stocks that the market has turned against. And the ones that might not make very much sense just because it's sort of a cyclical type of thing." For a more detailed discussion of value investing, as well as other investment philosophies, turn to chapter 3.

Michael also does his homework when picking each stock, researching not only the company itself but the industry in which it competes. "Basically I read about what the industry is. I find out what the growth potential is. I look at the competitors and see what their return on equity is and their return on assets, and I see what their profit margin is. Then I try to figure out if they're in line with the rest of the industry," he says. "I look at their products. I try to gauge how old the products are and if it seems like they have a good research and development department." Where does he find this kind of information? "The Web is incredible," he says. He gets data and real-time quotes off of several sites, including the site of his broker.

Like many investors Michael likes to think he can predict ups and downs in the market. His market timing has met with mixed success. A foray into several oil stocks doubled his money in a little over two years. But one of his early buys, into a small computer equipment manufacturer, showed him just what kind of risks he's taking with his money. He bought the stock at $14, and it promptly went up to $15. But then it went down, way down. He sold at $12, before the heavy bleeding started. Eight months later the stock was selling at 50 cents per share. "That was my first mistake," he says.

Measuring the true value of a stock can be a mysterious business, and finding the data can be just as tricky if you don't know where to look. Chapter 3 breaks down the financial numbers you can examine when picking stocks and offers a variety of sources to get you started. The chapter also examines various kinds of market risk and helps you work out your risk tolerance.

After building up a little investment experience, and confidence, Michael chose to buy into his investments using what is called a deep-discount broker. These brokers offer much cheaper trading fees, but they do not supply the kind of advice and hand-holding that a full-service broker can provide. Michael also shies away from buying

into stock mutual funds. "The thing I have against buying into stock funds, although I've done it in the past, is the amount of cost that the fund takes; it's always hard to gauge if it's reasonable or if it's at the expense of the gains you could make," he says.

Chapter 3 describes the different types of brokers you can hire and what kind of fees you'll be paying. You can also find out more about the fees associated with buying into mutual funds.

Michael also likes to shop for more than just stocks online. Recent buys include air-line tickets, and books for school. He always makes sure that the site he's shopping off of offers encryption technology to scramble his credit card number. He has some fear about letting his credit card information float around in cyberspace, but not enough to stop him. "I'm a little bit concerned but not really," he says. "If they can break into the Pentagon computer, nothing is really secure, I guess. Why don't they just break straight into Citibank's system and start pulling numbers?" For a look at the risks you take when you shop online turn to chapter 9.

Finally, deciding how much car insurance to carry is another personal finance choice that Michael had to figure out based on his own financial needs. "Since I have some money that could be taken from me if I were in an accident, I get way more cover-age than anything that could be taken from me. That's how you should look at it." To calculate your own insurance requirements for your car and other assets, flip to chapter 7.

What Do You Have to Protect?

Cash. Putting your money in the bank will prevent your cash from getting ripped off by burglars. Bank accounts are FDIC (Federal Deposit and Insurance Corporation) insured and they'll even earn a little interest. But they won't earn enough to protect your money from the ravages of inflation. You can prevent your money from depre-ciating by investing it in vehicles that offer higher rates of return. Also, a lawsuit could wipe out anything you save. Liability insurance can protect your money from legal surprises.

Investments. The stock market gives your money that extra earning power with the promise of higher interest. But stocks are susceptible to all kinds of uncertainties and the earnings will be taxed. You need to diversify and investigate the international landscape and alternative investments such as tax-free bonds, gold, and even art and collectibles.

Nest eggs for college and retirement. If you have kids, college will come sooner than you think. Vehicles such as Education IRAs, Lifetime Learning Credits, and the HOPE Scholarship Credit can help you to keep more of your money. Also, when planning your golden years, you'll find that not all retirement accounts are created equal. Some, such as 401(k)s, IRAs, and Keoghs, will protect your money from the IRS while you're socking it away. And Congress has recently added new retirement vehicles like the Roth IRA to meet your needs. How do you decide what's best?

Income and property. If something happened—an accident or an illness, for example—to prevent you from working, would you be able to meet your expenses? Protect your income with disability insurance. Also, your entire financial structure could be sabotaged if a fire, flood, or other natural disaster made it necessary for you to replace your belongings. Insurance—auto and homeowner's—protects your money from these dangers.

Your estate. It's never too early to start estate planning. Your family needs the money more if you die young than if you live to a ripe old age. Keep as much of it intact as you can by providing life insurance, making a will, setting up trusts, and gifting. Learn how to protect your money for the people you want to leave it to.

HOW *is* your money *At* RISK?

CHAPTER TWO

Throughout your lifetime, you and your money will face certain perils that threaten to separate you. It's not enough to plan your career, your finances, your retirement, and your estate.

As you map out your financial blueprint, take a look at how the risks outlined in this chapter can undermine your efforts.

Theft

At first blush the statistics can be scary. There were over 12 million property crime offenses in 1995, with over $15 billion lost, according to the Federal Bureau of Investigation. For burglary, the theft of $4.3 billion breaks down to a loss of $535 per victim. And for car theft, an average of $5,100 was stolen from 1.5 million unsuspecting drivers. In all, there were almost 14 million selected violent and

property crimes reported to law enforcement.

It's enough to make you want to move to a place like Steubenville, Ohio, Johnstown, Pennsylvania, or Appleton, Wisconsin, which are lucky enough to find themselves in the lowest 10 percent of crime areas. That compares to cities like Miami, Florida, which has over twice the overall national crime rate, and Tucson, Arizona, which is almost twice the average in both property and overall crime.

But the fact is the rate of crime—from burglary to car theft—has been going down for some time. For burglary, it's the lowest rate in 20 years. And the cities that get the worst rap for crime, like Los Angeles and Chicago, rank only about average, with about 6,000 overall crime offenses per 100,000 people. And metro areas like New York and Philadelphia are actually below the national average.

Telemarketing Fraud: Dialing for Dollars

Consumers lose $40 billion a year to telemarketing abuse. And the FBI estimates that there are 14,000 illegal telephone sales operations feeding off the trust of consumers every day. One recent example, reported by the Better Business Bureau, involves fraudulent telemarketers impersonating Bell Atlantic customer sales representatives. These phony reps offer to save you money by combining both your local and long-distance charges into one bill and offering discounts. Then they ask for personal information like your Social Security number. In other telemarketing scams, other personal data, like your credit card number or bank account number, is requested. Watch out. With this information in hand a crook can spend your money, either by ringing up charges on your Visa card or by withdrawing funds from your account.

Other telemarketing fraud involves persuasive reps who charm you into buying $5 junk jewelry sight unseen for $100. And then there are the many nonexistent sweepstakes offers that promise an exotic getaway. The problem here is that what gets away is your money.

Your first line of defense against these con artists is pretty straightforward:

- Be careful to whom you give your financial and other personal information. Don't give your credit card number (or expiration date), bank account number, Social Security number, or driver's license number to anyone you don't know. Remember, if someone has these numbers that person can become you—at least in a financial sense. And that means your money can easily become his or her money.

- Do business only with companies you know. If you aren't familiar with the firm, just ask them to send you brochures on who they are, how long they've been in business, and what products and services they offer. Legitimate companies are glad to do so.

- Resist pressure and take your time to decide. Disreputable telemarketers like the quick hit and hate to spend too much time with any one person. Besides, high-pressure sales tactics should be your red flag that the voice on the other end of your phone belongs to a con artist.

- Remember that you have weapons on your side. Under federal law you can tell telemarketers to stop calling and they must respect your wishes. If that doesn't do the trick, you can have your name put on a "don't call" list. Just contact the Direct Marketing Association's Telephone Preference Service (P.O. Box 9014, Farmingdale, NY 11735) and they'll do the rest. Finally, the most direct response always works best; just say "bahbye" and hang up the phone.

Investment Swindles

It can sound so easy. You are contacted by an "investment adviser" who wants you as a client. "Never invest with someone you don't know," he tells you, and he says he'll give you a free example of his "forecasting skill" before he ever asks to get paid.

He tells you to watch xyz stock because "my research department expects the stock to rise significantly." A few weeks pass and, sure enough, the price goes up. He then calls back; but once again he doesn't give you a sales pitch. Instead, he gives his second free sample. "My forecasters now tell me the price will come down." Once again, he's right! By now you're ready to give him serious money to invest. After all, if he was a con artist how could he have hit the financial bull's-eye twice?

Easy. Here's how it's done. The phony investment adviser starts with a calling list of, say, 200 people. In the first 100 calls he says xyz stock will go up. For the next 100 calls he says the stock will go down. If the stock's price goes up, he picks up the phone and calls the original 100 that got his "correct prediction." (If the stock's price had gone down, he simply would have called the other 100 on his list that got the "correct prediction.")

He then tells the first 50 in this original group that the price will now drop, and he tells the other 50 that the stock will continue to rise. The end result is that no matter what move the stock makes, the phony investment adviser now has a list of 50 true believers, ready to give him their life's savings.

Inflation

Your money is also at risk from a silent stalker. Each year every dollar you have loses more and more buying power because of inflation. For example, $130 could get you a year's tuition at the University of Iowa in 1947. By 1997, you needed $2,470 to get the same education in the Hawkeye State. The median home price in 1950 was around $7,500; today it's over $130,000.

Of course, you've heard all this "when I was your age you could get a Hershey bar for a nickel" before. But what you may not know is that inflation is a relatively new phenomenon.

It may be hard to believe, but at the onset of World War II in the 1940s a dollar still bought about as much as it had at the time of the U.S. Constitution's ratification in the 1780s. During the intervening 160 years, there were times when prices did increase (inflation) and still other times when prices came down (deflation), but there was no cumulative inflation.

It's only the generations since World War II that have had to worry about the value of their money eroding right before their eyes. The worst example of this came in the 1970s when inflation hovered around 15 percent. To put the insanity of that into perspective, just think about the year-end salary increase you get at your job, not including any special bonus. The increase, maybe 4 to 5 percent of your pay, is designed to keep your salary on par with inflation. Now imagine having to win a 15 percent bonus just to break even. Of course, most employers weren't that generous, and so people ended up with less disposable income. The effect on the cash sitting in bank accounts was equally brutal. The interest paid on saving accounts just couldn't keep up with 15 percent inflation; it was almost as bad as keeping your savings under your mattress.

Luckily, this scenario is merely a bad memory. Since the 1980s, inflation hasn't climbed above 6 percent—and for the past five years, inflation has been domesticated to a calm 3 percent.

But it's important to keep the memory of the 1970s in the back of your mind as you map out your personal financial plan. There's nothing to stop inflation from coming back to unsightly levels. That's why it's vital to put your money in investments that have historically outpaced inflation; instruments like large-company stocks, small-company stocks, mutual funds, and long-term government bonds, just to name a few. We'll take a look at these investments in chapter 3.

Credit Card Billing Errors

Your money is also at risk every time you go shopping. Maybe the department store took your credit card and accidentally charged you twice for the same item. Or maybe you've been billed for merchandise you returned or never received. In any event, you have the law on your side. In 1975, Congress passed the Fair Credit Billing Act (FCBA) to set up clear guidelines for consumers to get their money back. The law applies to credit card bills in the following cases:

Questions to Ask Financial Scammers

To protect yourself from investment scams, your best defense is to ask several questions:

- "Can you provide references?" The more legitimate the reference, like a well-known brokerage firm or bank, the more legitimate the investment adviser.

- "Can you send something in writing that explains in detail where you are, what your firm does, and how long you've been in business?" At that point you can do your own homework and check out the person's claims by calling local, state, and federal regulators, the Better Business Bureau.

- "Can I meet you at your office to discuss your offer?" By asking this question you can still weed out a lot of low-end scammers who operate out of so-called boiler rooms.

- "What risks are involved in your investment?" If the caller tells you there's no risk, hang up the phone. Remember, all investments have risks. If he doesn't know that, he may not be a con artist, but he's still too stupid to handle your money.

- "What government or industry regulatory supervision is your company subject to?" This question raises a red flag with swindlers. The last thing they want is to have to deal with regulators.

Where to Turn for Help in Fighting Scams

- If your complaint deals with scams over the telephone, contact the Federal Communications Commission at 1919 M St., NW, Washington, DC 20554, (202) 632-7553.

- For mail swindlers, see the Chief Postal Inspector, United States Postal Service, Washington, DC 20260, (202) 268-4267.

- Questions regarding stocks and other securities are handled by the Securities and Exchange Commission at 450 5th St., NW, Washington, DC 20006, (202) 728-8233, and by the National Association of Securities Dealers, 1735 K St., NW, Washington, DC 20006, (202) 728-8044.

You can also contact your state's attorney general. But remember that none of these resources can guarantee you any degree of satisfaction. You may have to go to court for any real resolution. In the end you have to be the first line of defense against scammers; ask lots of questions and always be cautious.

of the item in question because it's defective. The card issuer, in turn, can't report you as delinquent to a credit bureau or close your account until the dispute gets resolved or the case is settled in court. If it reaches that point you'll have to get an attorney. It's also important to note that defective merchandise to fall under the procedures just described for disputes, it generally has to be purchased within your home state or no more than 100 miles from your mailing address, and it has to cost more than $50.

Black Marks on Your Credit Report

Remember, your credit record can't be damaged merely because you dispute a charge. But there are many other ways that information in your credit report can affect you.

A bad credit report can hurt your chances of getting insurance, a mortgage, a loan, a credit card, even a job. Almost every adult (that means you) has a credit report. It includes data on where you live, work, whether you pay your bills on time, and whether you've been sued or arrested or have filed for bankruptcy. You've probably never seen your report, and that's too bad, because these files often contain inaccurate information.

The good news, once again, is that you have rights when it comes to these issues, and there are laws on the books to help you if you only follow a few simple steps. Remember, your rights are pretty much meaningless if you don't exercise them.

First, you have the right to peek inside your credit report. Any time you wish, the credit bureaus must offer up the information in your report, as well as a list of everyone who has recently requested it. Following are the addresses of the big three credit bureaus:

- Equifax—P.O. Box 740241, Atlanta, GA 30374-0241, (800) 685-1111

- Experian—P.O. Box 949, Allen, TX 75013, (800) 682-7654

- Trans Union—760 West Sproul Rd., P.O. Box 309, Springfield, PA 19064-0390, (800) 916-8800

The reports can cost up to $8, but they are free if you can prove that your report is inaccurate due to fraud.

Second, you must be told if the data in your credit report has been used against you. Businesses that deny you a loan or credit based on your report are required to provide you the name, address, and phone number of the credit bureau that gave the report.

When disputing inaccuracies remember to put everything in writing. In the sidebar you'll see a sample letter that should help you get started. The credit bureaus generally have a month to investigate the charges and then mail you a copy of their findings. If they rule in your favor, the bureaus must correct their reports and, if you ask, notify anyone who has recently requested your report.

If the bureau refuses to change its report, you have the right to add a brief statement to your file explaining the nature of the dispute. And if you can't get justice from these credit bureaus, you can sue them in state or federal court for violating the Fair Credit Reporting Act. If it gets that far, though, you'll need to put down this book and get yourself a good lawyer.

Lawsuits

Every time you drive your car, sign a contract, or even open your mouth, your money is at risk from lawsuits. Even your pets can get you sued. And if all this is depressing and you decide to relax with your clubs out on the links, you'd better watch out where you hit that golf ball. One golfer lost a suit for over $150,000 after a ball hit and permanently injured a bystander.

There are many different types of lawsuits. Simple suits that involve only small dollar amounts usually end up in small-claims court. You usually won't need a lawyer in these cases, but the threat to your wallet is still very real. In states like Rhode Island and Alabama, the dollar limit in small-claims court is only $1,500; but in other states, like Tennessee, you can face suits of $10,000 and over.

Other types of claims can cost you plenty—even if you win the case. That's because lawyer's fees, which are charged by the hour, as a percentage of the case's winnings,

or as a flat fee, don't come cheap. And while you always have the right to act as your own lawyer, that could be a foolish decision that costs you everything. So prepare to open up your checkbook.

Lawyers' hourly fees vary from state to state but can be around $100 to $200 an hour. A contingency fee is based on the assumption that you can win a case against someone else, say a business or other negligent party. The percentage you pay can be 30 percent of the award or higher, depending on how much legwork the attorney had to do for you.

Insurance can often help if you lose a suit. For example, you can buy auto insurance policies that will pay $100,000 to $300,000 to settle a claim. There is also homeowner's insurance and so-called umbrella policies that kick in if you end up having to pay out more than is covered by the standard auto or home policy. You can take a closer look at these insurance issues later in the book.

Love and Marriage

There are so many positive things about marriage that it's difficult to think of it as a risk to your money. But if you're married, or if you're planning to walk down the aisle with your sweetheart, you should be aware of a few potential problems—and their solutions.

When it comes to love and money, opposites really do attract. You and your honey may be of one mind when it comes to issues like career goals and children, but have you ever had a real discussion about the nuts and bolts of your personal finances? Do you know, for example, how much credit card debt your spouse is carrying? How about how much is still owed in college loans? Or what is spent each year on vacations or on a hobby?

It's important to tally up exactly how much debt each of you brings to the relationship. Then list your financial assets, such as your salaries, investments, and bank balances. Once you have a clear picture of what you're up against, it's easier to map out a strategy to pay down debt. That should avoid financial surprises early in the marriage and the bickering that can result.

You may also want to consider keeping separate bank accounts and credit cards. Some couples want to be truly together, both spiritually and financially. That's fine if it works for you. But having a joint account means you're both legally responsible for each other's debt. On the plus side, your combined assets can present a stronger case to a creditor if you're applying for a loan or a credit card.

But if one of you likes to live more extravagantly than the other, your best bet is to get separate accounts. That means you'll have your own credit history (and individual credit report), and you alone will be responsible for your spending sprees. Even if you go this route, it's still wise to consult your sweetheart if you're about to make any large purchases. Otherwise, things could get very ugly, very quickly. Also, you can always add a third account that pays for joint household expenses.

At tax time, many couples also have to worry about the so-called marriage penalty. If you're already married you may have run afoul of this quirk in the tax code. If you look at the standard deduction on your tax form, you'll see that it is different for couples. This often causes couples with roughly the same income to pay more in taxes than if they had filed as single. And if you're married, you can't file as being single.

In 1996, almost 21 million couples paid a marriage penalty, averaging about $1,400 apiece. Who said love was free? The penalty doesn't hit everyone equally, though. Couples with incomes of more than $50,000 are far more likely to pay extra. But only 12 percent of couples who make $20,000 or less paid any penalty at all.

The flip side to these differences in the tax laws is that many other married couples actually pay less to Uncle Sam—a marriage bonus. Couples that fit in this category generally have only one spouse bringing home a paycheck. About 25 million couples received a bonus in 1996, averaging $1,300. Again, income plays a role. Lower income couples are more likely to see a bonus check. As the number of dual-earning couples continues to rise, however, the marriage bonus will be more and more elusive.

In recent years Congress has talked about doing away with the marriage penalty. Of course, that's easier said than done. And even if they do banish it, what happens to the marriage bonus? There is a way to scrap one while saving the other, but that would mean the federal government would lose almost $30 billion in revenue, which would presumably have to come from somewhere else. Anyway, you see the dilemma. In any case, there are several bills before Congress that would allow couples simply to choose whether they want to file their tax form as married or single. And if that sounds good to you, just call up your elected representatives and tell them what's what.

Downturns in the Economy

Stocks are up, interest rates are down, and the economy continues to chug along. Why worry? Because even in good economic times layoffs have recently been averaging about half a million per year. The days when you could get hired straight out of college by a top company like IBM, work hard, and stick around long enough to collect the gold watch are long since over.

Many who have faced the downsizing ax describe the experience as surprising and emotionally painful. And that doesn't include the financial pain. If you're laid off, you should be aware that the average severance package pays out only one or two weeks salary for each year of your service. If you haven't been there long, that's not much of a parachute. Plus, the government considers this cash as salary, so 30 percent or more of it will go to pay for income and Social Security taxes. Also, you can kiss your employer's health insurance plan good-bye. As an added bonus, any retirement plan money you might have accumulated at work, like a 401(k), will have to be moved out of the company's account and into yours.

We will talk in more detail about health insurance and 401(k) issues later in the book. But just to let you know that things are not as gloomy as the picture just painted, there are solutions and strategies to help out. As far as health insurance is concerned, federal law allows most departing employees at most companies to keep their employer's health coverage for up to 18 months after the layoff ax falls. The catch is you have to pay the full premium. And when it comes to your 401(k) payout, if you immediately roll the cash into an Individual Retirement Account you can avoid hefty taxes and still have the option of later on moving the investment into your new employer's 401(k) plan. See chapters 5 and 6 for more information.

Bankruptcy: Thinking the Unthinkable

The option of last resort is to seek protection from your creditors under federal bankruptcy laws. Unfortunately, bankruptcy has become all too common. Every year more than one million Americans choose this option. Last year, that number jumped to 1.3 million, an all-time high. There's a real price you'll pay if you make this decision. Your credit record will be tarnished for up to ten years and you may find it difficult later on to get a mortgage or credit.

You may want to talk with a credit counselor or an attorney beforehand, but basically, bankruptcy for individuals comes in two flavors: Chapter 7 and Chapter 13.

Chapter 7 bankruptcy involves liquidating most of your assets to settle your debts and make a fresh start. Chapter 13 bankruptcy deals with reorganizing your debt so you can pay off your creditors. Once you file a bankruptcy petition, creditors are prevented from starting or continuing most legal proceedings against you. However, some debts, like most taxes, alimony, child support, and student loans cannot be forgiven or discharged. For more information you can click on the American Bankruptcy Institute's home page (http://www.abiworld.org).

It's also important to note that bankruptcy costs you even if you're in great financial shape and never need to file for Chapter 7 or 13. Every American household pays on average $400 a year in higher prices and higher interest rates because of the costs associated with personal bankruptcies.

Sample Letter to Dispute Data in Your Credit Report

Inaccurate information in your credit report can really hurt you. If you're trying to buy a home, for example, a bad report can be the kiss of death. So get a copy of your report and look it over. Here's a sample letter you can use if your report is wrong through no fault of your own. The letter is based on information provided by the Federal Trade Commission.

Complaint Department
Name of Credit Reporting Agency
Address

Dear Sir or Madam:

I am writing to dispute the following information in my file. The items I dispute also are encircled on the attached copy of the report I received. (Identify the items disputed by name of source, such as creditors or tax court, and identify the type of item, such as a credit account, or judgment against you.) This item is (inaccurate/incomplete) because (describe what is inaccurate or incomplete and why). I am requesting that the item be deleted (or whatever action you want taken) to correct the information.

Enclosed are copies of (list any documents that back up your claim) supporting my position. Please reinvestigate this matter and (delete or correct) the disputed items as soon as possible.

Sincerely,
(your name)

Enclosures: (list what you are enclosing)

Most of the information on your report can stay there for up to seven years. Bankruptcy data can be reported for ten years. And there's no time limit for information requested in connection with an application for a job that makes over $75,000 a year, or a credit line or life insurance policy of $150,000 or more.

If you contact the credit bureau you can opt out of having your credit information sent to credit or insurance companies who routinely retrieve the data to make unsolicited offers. The request will be honored for two years. If you want something a little more permanent, you can ask for and sign a special "opt-out" form to get you off these unsolicited lists forever.

A final note. If you find yourself the victim of an incorrect credit report, you might be contacted by a credit repair service promising to solve all your problems—for just a small fee. There are a few things to watch out for. First off, it's illegal for these services to ask for payment until after your credit report is fixed or otherwise dealt with. It's also illegal to change any negative data that is accurate; so don't believe a repair service that tells you differently. And third, it's illegal for these services to fix your credit file using "file segregation," a trick where they make you a second credit report by using, for example, a second Social Security number.

Remember, you have the power (and the legal right) to fix your file yourself. Yes, it will take some time and effort, but that's the deal. And even if you have negative information in your report that's not removable, you still have options. Say you missed a few payments last year because of a sudden illness or because you were briefly unemployed; you can write to the credit bureau and have this short explanation inserted into your file. This tactic can also be helpful if your report shows that you owe debt because the item in question was defective. If the explanation makes sense, it may wipe away any black mark on your good name.

Taxes and the IRS

Even if you get a refund check every year, your money is still at risk from the Internal Revenue Service. That's because the byzantine tax code almost forces you to pay for professional assistance to put your forms together correctly.

Taxpayers currently spend over $100 billion a year for hired tax help, ranging from H&R Block to high-priced tax attorneys. Add to that the time and money it takes to keep records, as well as fill out, file, and process the tax forms. The tax code is immense (every year 300,000 trees are felled to produce IRS forms and instructions), with myriad sections, subsections, loopholes, and vagaries to trip you up.

Although the Federal government has recently been in a tax-cutting mood, the fact is that all through the 1990s your taxes have been going up. In 1992, for example, the so-called tax-free day (the date by which the average American earns enough to pay off all federal, state, and local taxes) fell on April 30. Last year, the date was bumped up to May 9.

Of course, you're not average; and it's important to note that your hit by taxes often depends on what region of the country you call home. When it comes to state taxes, states like Florida, Texas, and New Hampshire pay no income taxes. Other states, like California and Ohio charge rates of up to 9 percent of your income. And if you live in New York City, fuhgeddaboudit. They get you for up to 11 percent.

Luckily, there is some good news. Congress and the president came together last year to cut taxes outright, as well as offer new tax loopholes that many of you can use to your advantage.

For starters, they've lowered taxes on the capital gains you pay when you sell stocks or mutual funds you've had for over 18 months for a profit. If you're single, with an income of less than $25,350, as of 1998 you'll have to give only 10 percent of your profit (down from 15 percent) to the IRS. If you make more, the rate is 20 percent (down from 28 percent). And if you're married and file jointly, you can make up to $42,350 and still get the 10 percent rate. Also, the capital gains tax rate on most homes sold after May 7, 1997 is now 0 percent. Not bad.

This new tax-free status applies to the first $500,000 in profit you make when you sell your home.

If you have kids and meet certain income requirements, Uncle Sam will now pony up a $400 per child tax credit. The full credit applies to couples filing jointly, with incomes below $110,000, and to singles who make less than $75,000. That should work for most of you. The credit phases out if you make more. In English, it means $2,500 in taxes, will now have to cough up only $1,300—a 48 percent tax cut.

Another new child-friendly break deals with college costs. Starting January 1, 1998, families can get a $1,500 tax credit for each of the first two years of postsecondary education, or a $1,000 break for any year of college.

The final two tax improvements concern something that may be decades away from you but is still of vital importance today: retirement. Individual Retirement Accounts (IRAs), which we will take a more detailed look at in chapter 5, are a great way to build wealth while keeping the IRS at bay. If you qualify, you can deduct from your taxes up to $2,000 in contributions that you put into an IRA. And that cash grows tax-free until you retire. It used to be that you couldn't make more than $25,000 a year and still be eligible for the full break. Now you can make $30,000 and still qualify.

But these adjustments might seem trivial when compared to the creation of a new breed of IRA that holds special advantages. It's called the Roth IRA, and it allows singles making less than $95,000 and couples making less than $150,000 to contribute the same $2,000 that they would put into a traditional IRA—but with a twist. Upon retirement you pay nothing in taxes. The only catch is you can't deduct from your taxes your yearly $2,000 contributions. That's a concession worth taking as long as you don't expect your income tax bracket to fall sharply, say from 28 to 15 percent, once you retire.

So now you know what's new out there. The only downside to these new tax breaks and loopholes is that they add still more complexity to the tax code and further guarantee that you'll have to hire help to fill out all your tax forms.

Watch out for problems that can foul up your tax return. The most common mistakes include not signing your return, incorrect math, and failure to include all required information, like W-2 forms. These forms are the wage and tax statements that you receive from your employer. Each employer that you have in a year must send you a W-2. If you don't get one in the mail by February 1, call them.

If you have investment income, such as from mutual funds, you'll also receive a 1099 form. The same rules for getting the forms apply here. It is vital that you obtain all this paperwork before filling out your tax forms. If you fail to report all your income you could end up with an unfriendly visit from the IRS.

Audits

You are now officially entering hell. Please keep your hands and elbows inside the vehicle. An audit is supposed to be merely an impartial review of your tax return to make sure all your information is complete and accurate. But the truth is that the burden of proof concerning your innocence is on you, not on the IRS. If, for example, you donated $200 worth of clothes and expect to deduct that from your taxes, you must get a receipt as proof. The IRS does not have to prove that you didn't make the donation.

Some people are more likely to get audited than others. If you're a lawyer, an accountant, or a doctor, watch out and be extra careful. Also, if you take large deductions, the IRS is going to want to see a detailed paper trail of receipts as verification.

Some audits are simple. If you forget to include a minor piece of information, the IRS may just do a correspondence audit, where all you have to do is mail in the missing documents and that's that. But other audits require you to show up at an IRS field office with your forms and documents. If it gets that far, you should consider asking your tax preparer to accompany you to the audit.

If you're found to be at fault, you will get a letter that gives you 30 days to either agree with the finding of the audit or appeal. The letter will also explain what steps you need to take depending on your choice of action. At this stage you don't have a lot of good options, which is why it's so important to keep thorough documentation.

Government Regulations

These regulations are a double-edged sword. On the one hand, public health, safety, and environmental regulations, as well as labor laws and property rights infringements, can cost you plenty. In fact, federal regulations cost you almost $700 billion a year; that's $2,800 per person. You see these costs both in higher income taxes and in the taxes you pay on big-ticket items like your car. On the other hand, nobody wants to get rid of regulations that provide for clean air, clean water, and food and workplace safety. So there's the rub.

These costs have risen sharply over the past 30 years. For example, the costs of so-called social regulations, which include health and environmental rules, have almost tripled since the 1970s, from $80 billion to $220 billion today. Of course, this has been good economic news for government employees; full-time regulatory staff has increased from 70,000 to 128,500 in 25 years.

And the *Code of Federal Regulations*, the book that holds all federal regulations, now fills up almost 140,000 pages—10,000 of which were added during the first term of the Clinton administration.

But recently there has been some reducing of government red tape. Since 1994, Congress has taken a new look at federal regulations and decided that some could be cut back. They've begun to deregulate both the agriculture and telecommunications industries. And they're currently talking about deregulating the electric utility industry.

These measures promise to put money in your pocket, both by lowering the cost of the goods that previously fell under regulation (such as the food you put on your table and the rates you pay for cable TV) and by possibly cutting your taxes, due to the theory that a smaller government needs less funds to keep it running.

Congress has also made an effort to stem the tide of so-called unfunded mandates, which happens when states and localities must implement federal rules without receiving any federal funds to offset the costs. These new unfunded mandate savings should also trickle down to your wallet in the form of lower state and local taxes.

Your ATM Card—Use It Properly

Automatic teller machines (ATMs) have been around only since the late 1960s, but already they're an indispensable part of our lives. They give us financial options that our grandparents could only dream about. Today you can roam around from Asia to Europe to Latin America and use your ATM card as easily as when you walk to your local bank. You can fly to London, whip out your ATM card, and get $100 worth of British pounds withdrawn at the machine to begin your shopping spree.

ATM cards have special advantages over other methods of payment, such as credit cards. As is painfully obvious every month when you open up your credit card statement, cards like Visa and American Express inflict interest charges on unpaid balances. ATMs do not. They automatically take from your account what you withdraw at the machine. Of course, the banks can hit you with a fee, maybe $1 to $3, every time you use their card at an ATM. But there is a way around that.

You can save money and avoid paying ATM fees if you do a little homework and know where to use your card. First off, financial institutions that engage in charging ATM fees are required to disclose how much they charge. So call around, and find the ATMs in your area that don't assess a surcharge.

A second trick is that you can often avoid ATM fees when you're buying groceries. Many large supermarkets, such as Safeway, Giant, and Food Lion, will let you buy your food using an ATM card and not charge you the customary fee. And some stores will even let you get cash back at the point of sale for free—saving you a trip to your bank.

Just as important when using your ATM is to avoid making foolish mistakes that can cost you money. There are more than 200 million ATM cards floating around today in the United States, and they are a prime target of thieves. A little common sense is your best protection.

When picking a personal identification number (PIN), for example, don't choose anything obvious, like your birthday or part of your address. Also, always take the receipt the ATM machine spits out every time you make a withdrawal. The information on that card could help a thief gain access to your account. And it's a good idea to use your hand to shield the screen when you're punching in your PIN. Otherwise, wandering eyes may figure out your number.

If all these precautions fail and you still get ripped off, be sure to exercise your legal rights. If you report your ATM card as lost or stolen within two business days of discovering the loss, and report immediately any unauthorized uses that show up on your bank's monthly statement, your liability is limited to $50. Otherwise, you could be responsible for up to $500 in unauthorized charges.

TAX TIPS

- Public libraries have tax forms.

- Use the envelope provided by the IRS in the instruction booklet.

- Round money amounts to the nearest dollar.

- Use your forms from last year as a guide.

- Keep a copy of your completed return and other tax documents for at least three years.

- When you make out your check to the IRS, spell out "Internal Revenue Service." The initials "IRS" can easily be changed to "MRS" (and then somebody's name) by a scammer if your letter is stolen.

- Go to the IRS's Web site (http://www.irs.ustreas.gov) for more tax information and advice.

A Final Note

This chapter was designed to show you how your money is at risk. Unfortunately, that could be the subject of an entire book. But suffice it to say that

whether it's scams or poor spending decisions that are at issue, you have to be your own best defense. You have to do your homework, find out about the people and firms you do business with, and be ready to exercise your legal rights.

When making purchases, try not to hurry. Some of the worst personal finance mistakes you can make are pretty easy to avoid if you just sit down for a moment and think things through. Don't sign anything unless it is completely filled out and you've read all the fine print. Examine the merchandise carefully. Check warranties. Keep receipts and warranty information. And ask about return policies in advance.

You can't be clueless about your money.

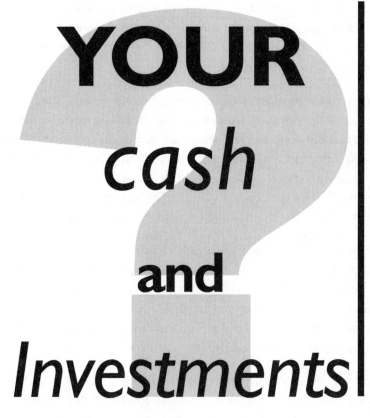

YOUR *cash* and *Investments*

CHAPTER THREE

The easiest way to protect your cash from theft is to plunk it in the bank. But the interest rate you'll get won't be much better than the rate of inflation, so there's got to be a better choice for most of your money.

In this chapter we will look at banks and credit unions as places to keep your "operating cash"; we will explain the way to find the best credit card to keep your expenses down; and most important, we will examine the investment alternatives for the rest of your cash to help you get a higher rate of return on your money.

Banks versus Credit Unions

Credit unions on average offer the lowest fees and pay the most competitive rates on savings and checking accounts. They also charge lower rates on loans and credit cards than do banks. And most credit unions offer free checking with no minimum balance.

Just compare credit union offers with what you get with your basic checking service. Banks were recently averaging 1.15 percent annually on interest-bearing checking accounts. Credit unions beat that by a mile, averaging 2.08 percent, according to Bank Rate Monitor.

It's no wonder that there are more than 70 million people in credit unions. The catch is that not everyone can sign up with a credit union. You need to have a "common bond" with the credit union you want to join, such as a common occupational, association, or community affiliation. For example, many large employers have credit unions. The reason credit unions have such an advantage is that banks are forced to fight with one hand tied behind their back. Credit unions currently enjoy the competitive advantages of federal tax exemption and less stringent regulations.

Lately, though, the nation's 11,500 credit unions have experienced setbacks. The Supreme Court recently ruled that some credit unions have expanded their membership to beyond those with a common bond. And that has put those members at risk of having to pull their money out. Legislation is moving through Congress right now to reverse the high court's decision, but nothing is guaranteed. So if you join a credit union, be sure that you really do have a legitimate reason for belonging.

Banks, in their defense, do offer some advantages over credit unions. One is a greater selection of financial services. Most credit unions are concerned with basic banking and check-writing services and usually won't offer the wide array of mutual funds and other investment products that banks have started to supply in abundance. Banks also are usually more convenient to get to; there's always one just a few blocks down the street.

Before you make any final decision on whom to bank with, visit the institution, ask questions, and get plenty of brochures and other documentation of what is offered and what fees you'll pay. That way you can compare all the services that are important to you, including fees for cashier's checks, safe-deposit box rentals, and ATM use, as well as the interest rates on loans and deposit accounts. Of all the questions you'll ask, these three may be the most important:

• "How much do I have to keep on deposit each month, and how many

checks can I write, without paying a fee?" You should also try to flush out just what types of accounts the bank offers, ranging from "no frills" accounts to "packaged" services.

- "Can you give me a brochure on what types of loan and investment products you offer?" If you want more than basic checking privileges, this question could make the difference in your decision.

- "What are your hours and what days are you closed?" If you're planning to do your banking on the weekends, you'd better make sure it's open. After all, the expression that someone works "banker's hours" exists for a reason.

Handling Your Savings

Once you've chosen either a bank or a credit union, you need to think about what services you need from that institution. After all, why put any of your money in a bank or credit union that's only going to pay interest equal to, or less than, inflation? Most of your money should be invested elsewhere, such as in mutual funds and other products that we'll get into later in this chapter and in the rest of the book.

You should stash only enough money in your bank to handle your need for ready cash and to cover six months living expenses, should you meet an unexpected downsizing at work. This money is your "operating cash." Always put safety first in choosing who will take care of this emergency money: Look only at banks that are insured by the Federal Deposit Insurance Corporation (FDIC) and credit unions that are backed by the National Credit Union Administration (NCUA). This will protect up to $100,000 of your money should the financial institution go belly-up.

To start with, you'll probably need a checking account. This is the cornerstone of most people's easy-access savings. Every year, 65 billion checks are processed in the United States. With a checking account, you will have instant access to your money, either by writing a check or by punching a few buttons at an ATM. You may or may not be paid interest on this account, and you may have restrictions as to how many checks you can write or how many ATM withdrawals you can make per month. Savings accounts are another consideration; they pay better interest than checking

accounts but come with more restrictions. They are also one of the most popular services that banks offer, with 70 percent of adults in the United States participating.

Banks and credit unions also provide loans for home buying and car purchases. And banks take care of retirement planning by setting up IRAs and 401(k)s. Chapter 5 is the place to go for that information.

For the investment-minded, banks and credit unions provide still higher rates of return with certificates of deposit, also called CDs. These financial instruments are insured up to $100,000, and yield enough to beat inflation. The rules are you have to leave your money in the CD for the agreed upon time period, which ranges from a month to five years; otherwise you pay a penalty. You can buy CDs in denominations of as little as $500, and as much as $10,000. Basically, you earn more with CDs that have longer time periods and greater denominations.

Another instrument you can put your money into is a money market deposit account, or MMDA. Don't confuse these accounts with money market mutual funds, which offer better rates but don't come with FDIC insurance. MMDAs let you write a limited number of checks each month against your account and make certain withdrawals without penalty. They give you more accessibility to your money than CDs, but you'll generally get lower interest because of this convenience.

Money market mutual funds are probably a better choice. These funds are basically large pools of investor money managed by an investment company. For a minimum requirement of $1,000, this type of fund invests in short-term instruments, such as CDs, short-term corporate bonds, and short-term government bonds. You can sell your shares in the fund when you wish, and there are no sales fees for buying or selling your fund. The only cost is a small management fee.

Securities from the U.S. Treasury offer the safety of the federal government. While they are still subject to market risks like changing interest rates, you can be sure that there will be no default. You can buy them at your bank at a variety of maturities, ranging from three months to one year. Or you can save money and avoid the middleman by buying them directly from Uncle Sam. But because the minimum amount needed to go this route is $10,000, it's probably not a realistic choice for most of us.

Picking the Right Credit Card and Using It Wisely

Before we get into the nitty-gritty of investing, let's first talk a little about finding the right credit card for your needs. One of the reasons many people give for why they can't starting investing in stocks and other securities is because they don't have any extra money left after they pay off their debts. And much of that debt is credit card debt. That's a shame, considering that many people are currently carrying around credit cards with higher than average interest rates, not to mention the fees.

There are steps you can take to find the best card for you. In the same way that we all have different telephone calling patterns, we all have different credit card using habits. So the same rules for long-distance plan shopping apply here: Do your homework and find out who offers what.

If you're like most people, you're constantly getting credit card offers in the mail saying "Congratulations," you have been "preapproved for our card," which luckily for you has a "superlow rate," but you have to act fast "before the offer expires." The cards may be from banks you've never heard of, or they may be affiliated with clubs you belong to or even your alma mater. All these choices can be overwhelming, and it's hard to know what to do.

Even though credit cards came into existence only 40 years ago, they are now part of the fabric of our financial lives. Credit cards can pay for meals, appliances, clothing, schooling, vacations—anything you can think of.

Before you select a credit card (or before you check to see if your current credit card is right for you) you should be familiar with the jargon of the credit industry. Under the Fair Credit and Charge Discount Disclosure Act, you have the right to compare all the terms and fees that the various card issuers are offering you. So get their terms in writing. That way you'll be able to compare apples to apples.

In the forms you get from a credit card issuer, the key terms to consider are the card's annual percentage rate, annual fee, grace period, and transaction fees and other charges. You will also need to know the issuer calculates any finance charges.

The annual percentage rate, or APR, is given to you when you apply for a card, when you open your account, and every time you receive your bill. The APR is basically the cost of credit, expressed as a yearly rate. The card issuer also will disclose its "periodic rate," which is what it applies to any outstanding account balance you have in order to figure the finance charge for each billing period.

The interest rate the credit card charges might be variable or fixed. A variable rate changes over time because the rate is tied to an index, such as the prime rate, six-month Treasury bill rate, or the Federal Reserve discount rate. So, for example, if you have a credit card that charges "prime + 3," you know that the interest you'll fork over on your unpaid balances can go up or down with the prime rate. Fixed rates are not tied to these indexes, so they avoid the roller coaster ride.

Be wary of the "introductory rates" you see in big red letters on your credit card junk mail. The rate may be quite low and seem too good to believe. And you would be right. Most of the superlow rates that suck you in last for only six months, maybe a year. Then you'll have to start paying the normal rate, which can be higher than other cards that you could have gone with. So look for the full rate when making comparisons.

Many credit card issuers charge you an annual fee merely for the privilege of carrying their card. These fees can range from $25 to $50 for most cards, and from $70 on up for "gold" cards. But many other cards don't impose an annual fee. So look around, and don't just accept that you have to pay one.

A card's "grace period" is the time between the date of a purchase and the date interest starts being charged on that purchase. Normal credit cards give you 25 to 30 days of grace, just long enough so you can pay off your balances each billing period without being stuck with interest charges. Some cards give you no grace, so interest begins to accrue from the moment you make your purchase. Stay away from these cards like the plague.

Some card companies charge transaction fees, such as when you use your card to get a cash advance, or when you fail to make a payment on time, or when you go over your credit limit. Be sure to note these fees.

If your card doesn't have a grace period, or if you're the kind of credit card user who lets charges lapse over billing periods, you should look closely at the fine print on the forms you get from the credit companies. There you will find their computation method for finance charges. How a credit issuer computes your finance charge can really make a difference in how much you'll pay, even when the APR for that issuer is the same as with another card. The three ways a credit card issuer can compute the charges are with the average daily balance, the adjusted balance, or the previous balance.

The most common method used is the average daily balance. Here you get credit for your payment from the day the card company gets it. To calculate the balance due, the company totals the beginning balance for each day in the billing period and subtracts any payments credited to your account that day. The resulting daily balances are totaled up for the billing cycle and that total is then divided by the number of days in the billing period.

Usually the most advantageous method for you is the adjusted balance. This is computed by subtracting the payments you made during the present billing period from the balance you owed at the end of the previous period. You have until the end of the billing cycle to pay part of your balance, and you avoid the interest charges on that part.

With the previous balance method, the balance is the amount that you owed at the end of the previous billing cycle. Payments and purchases made during the current billing period are not taken into account.

Now that you know some of the terms of the credit card trade, you can figure out what type of card you need. Not all the key terms you've just seen are equally important to you. It all comes down to how you use your card and how you deal with debt. For example, if you always pay off your monthly bill in full, you don't need to be as concerned about getting the super low interest rate. The issues that are most important for you are that the card have no annual fee and have an ample grace period.

Doing your homework researching different credit cards can take time, but the money you'll saving picking the right one should be incentive enough. Say you have $2,500 in credit card debt, which is about the national average, and you pay an APR of 18 percent, with an annual fee of $20. The amount you'd pay in finance charges

annually would be $450; and $470 if you include the $20 fee. Lowering the APR by just a few points, along with finding a card with no annual fee, can give you decent savings. With an APR of 14 percent, the finance charge drops to $350. So is a little effort on your part worth $120? What do you think?

Investing: The Risks

The first thing to remember is that all investments have risks. There are many valuable investment options out there, including stocks, bonds, and mutual funds. If you ever hope to gain a certain amount of financial freedom, these investments are your best ticket. Also, if you start investing in your twenties, you have the time to be aggressive and take some risks.

But all this must be tempered by a firm awareness that what you're doing carries risk, not only that you may not make as much as you expect but that you could lose every cent you put in. So before you jump into the wonderful (and dangerous) world of investing, take a look at the following disclaimer.

The money you put into stocks, mutual funds, and other types of investments should come from a pile that is separate from what goes into your savings. Investment money is long-term money, meaning you must be prepared not to touch the cash for a period of years. You also have to be prepared to see your investments go down in value, sometimes way down. "Markets go up, markets go down," is one of the oldest truths in investing, no matter how rosy things look now. There are profits out there, but there are also risks.

The greater the potential is for profit, the greater the risk. One of the most important parts of managing your investments is to understand the relationship between risk and reward. Every investor has his or her own tolerance level for risk. You need to think about what you're comfortable with. You also need to set in your mind what your time frame is for each investment. Do you need the money to pay for something three months or 30 years down the road? Again, the more time you have, the more flexibility you have to deal with and recover from risk.

If your tolerance level is high, you may want to buy stock in companies that your research and instincts tell you are ripe for big profits. Over the past 70 years, stocks on average have returned 10 to 15 percent annually. Of course, the stocks you pick may or may not meet that average. Stocks are inherently volatile because their prices are set by millions of investors, large and small, all over the world. If you invest, say, $1,000 in a stock, your investment will rise or fall depending in large part on the rise and fall of that stock's price. Keep in mind that there are many risks for stocks that can affect their price, including:

1. The company may be a good company that is badly managed.

2. The company may be a bad company (in an industry that is declining) that no amount of good management can help.

3. The company may be good and the management may be good, but stock analysts, money managers, and investors may hate it anyway and just decide to sell en masse. This risk is one that small high-tech stocks are especially prey to; they often get hammered at the slightest hint of bad news.

4. The company and management may be good but may be in a sector of the economy that's in a slump. Or maybe the overall economy is in recession.

This list is just a sample. You may feel you don't want to be that risky. Maybe bonds are a better choice for you. On average, bonds don't give you as good a return on your investment as stocks, but they do tend to deliver a more predictable stream of income. But again, keep in mind the risks:

1. High interest rates and inflation can hit bonds.

2. Even if interest rates are low, the company issuing the bond can default.

3. Even if interest rates are low and the company doesn't default, the firms that rate a company's likelihood of default can give the company a poor grade for financial stability.

Risk is everywhere, both real and imagined. There is a lot of self-fulfilling prophecy in the investment world. And it's hard to know what's going on around you at any

Where to Get Information on Credit Cards

There are a number of valuable resources that you can tap into to find the best card, and most are free. The Federal Reserve System collects information on the key terms we've discussed in this chapter for hundreds of credit card issuers and then lists it all free for your perusal. Just click on to their Web site (http://www.borg.frb.fed.us/pubs/shop/). The downside is that the data can be almost a year old, so if you find a card that you really like, you'll have to call the company to confirm that the terms are still current.

Another good Web site is run by Bank Rate Monitor (http://www.bankrate.com). They have a computer worksheet where you input the key terms that are most important to you (like not having an annual fee or wanting a long grace period) and they show you current information on the top cards in those categories. The site also gives consumer information and how-to advice on buying and using a card.

If you still need more information on credit issues, you can turn to Bankcard Holders of America (BHA), an independent, nonprofit group. This group is funded almost entirely by its 50,000 members, who pay a membership fee of $24 a year. Members of BHA receive about two dozen publications put out by the consumer group, as well as a bimonthly newsletter. The publications are also available to consumers who are not members for a small fee. They include brochures on topics such as the best low-rate credit cards, the best rebate/frequent flyer cards, consumer rights, and how to rebuild credit. A complete list of publications is available by writing to Bankcard Holders of America at: 524 Branch Drive, Salem, VA 24153. Include a stamped, self-addressed envelope.

When you've finally found the card that's right for you, there are a few points to remember if you want to use the card wisely:

- Keep copies of sales slips so you can compare credit card charges when your bill arrives.

- Rip up or keep the carbon copies from the sales slips you sign using a credit card.

- Never lend your card to a friend or give your credit card number over the phone to any company that you don't know.

- Don't use a cordless or cellular phone when making credit purchases since those calls can be intercepted by scanners.

You need to know where your card is at all times and who has your number, because if a criminal ever obtained your card or number that person could easily ring up charges on your account. If you end up with unauthorized uses, be sure to exercise your rights under the Fair Credit Billing Act, explained in chapter 2. And be sure to report your stolen card to the card issuer immediately as soon as you realize it's gone. The number you need to call is often listed on your monthly billing statement. If you report the loss before the card is used, the card issuer cannot hold you responsible for the charges. But if the card is used before you make the report, you can be held liable for up to $50 worth of unauthorized card charges.

one time. So maybe the answer is to hand your investment money over to a mutual fund, where you'll have an experienced manager to shepherd your cash to bigger and better profits. Or at least that's the theory.

Mutual funds are large pools of investor money that are handled by one or several managers. Mutual funds buy groups of stocks, or bonds, or a mixture of the two. Mutual funds are a great idea in that they offer historically high returns with relatively little work on your part. But, of course, mutual funds carry the same risks that are associated with the stocks and/or bonds that they buy. In addition, mutual funds have their own unique risks, including:

1. Your mutual fund's "star" manager could jump ship, leaving your money to be managed by somebody you don't have confidence in.

2. The fund could become a victim of its own success. If a small mutual fund becomes wildly popular, literally billions of dollars from new investors can flood into the manager's hands; and he or she may not be able to handle it all. In other words, a large fund can't move in and out of investments as quickly as a small fund, and that can hamper results.

3. There's a saying that even a broken clock is right twice a day. You could end up with a mutual fund whose manager may have been hot when you bought into the fund but who was just lucky and is now lagging behind the competition.

There is another risk you must consider, perhaps the most important—the risk of not investing, or investing so late in life that you're forced to take unnecessary risks to try to catch up. As we've mentioned before, if you leave all your money tied up in a bank (or under your mattress), it is still at risk from the silent stalker of inflation. Over the years, inflation will eat away at the value of what money you have.

If you're just starting out in your career, you may not have much money at this point, but you do have time on your side. If you start today, make investing a habit, and make consistent purchases into, say, a stock mutual fund, you can make compounding work for you.

The Federal Government Can Help You

If you need federal help in dealing with credit card transactions, there are specific organizations you can contact, depending on the type of business that issued you the card.

- For state member banks of the federal reserve system, write to: Consumer and Community Affairs, Board of Governors of the Federal Reserve System, 20th & C Sts., NW, Washington, DC 20551.

- For national banks, write to: Comptroller of the Currency, Compliance Management, Mail Stop 7-5, Washington, DC 20219.

- For federal credit unions, write to: National Credit Union Administration, 1776 G St., NW, Washington, DC 20456.

- For nonmember federally insured banks, write to: Office of Consumer Programs, Federal Deposit Insurance Corporation, 550 17th St., NW, Washington, DC 20429.

- For federally insured savings and loans and federally chartered state banks, write to: Consumer Affairs Program, Office of Thrift Supervision, 1700 G St., N.W., Washington, DC 20552.

- For other credit card issuers, such as retail and gasoline companies, write to: Division of Credit Practices, Bureau of Consumer Protection, Federal Trade Commission, Washington, DC 20580.

Here's what that means: If you invest $100 a month every month for the next 5 years and end up earning 10 percent annually, you'll see your cash grow to around $7,800. Not bad, but look what happens as the years pile up. If you keep up the same investment habit for 10 years, the money will go to over $20,600. Stay the course for 20 years, and you'll see it jump to more than $76,500. And at the end of 30 years, you can celebrate a gain of almost $300,000.

A long-term 10 percent annual return on your investment is fairly reasonable, considering how stocks have done over the past 70 years and especially how well things have been over the past 20 years. But let's say you wait to start investing. Let's say you wait until you're in your thirties or forties, when most Baby Boomers figured out that they had to start investing. At that age, you're going to have to find investments with average returns a lot higher than 10 percent or invest much more than $100 a month if you want to build a six-figure nest egg.

Stocks: An Introduction

When you buy stock in a company, what you're actually doing is buying part ownership in that company. Of course, it's only a very small part. Large companies can have millions of shares. If the price of those shares goes up, you make money. If the price goes down, you lose money. It's that simple. In addition, most companies pay out dividends to their shareholders, so you see some income on top of any appreciation in the stock's price.

Stocks and stock markets in this country have been around since the eighteenth century. Today, the main stock markets are the New York Stock Exchange (NYSE), the American Stock Exchange (AMEX), and the Nasdaq National Market System. There are also regional exchanges in major cities like Chicago, Denver, and Los Angeles.

There are plenty of stocks to choose from. There are over 4,000 stocks traded by Nasdaq, including high-tech companies like Microsoft and Apple Computer. The NYSE lists more than 3,000 companies, including such well-established firms as IBM and Coca-Cola. And the AMEX lists over 1,000 stocks.

Each stock's performance is different, but on average, stocks have historically given investors a great ride. Over the past 70 years, which includes the Great Depression and numerous recessions, the compound annual return of stocks in small companies has exceeded 12 percent. For large companies, the return has been slightly lower but still impressive at more than 10 percent. That more than beats inflation, which historically comes in averaging just over 3 percent.

When you first start investing you will hear all sorts of terms being thrown around to describe and classify stocks, and you might not know what it all means. But once you understand the jargon of the stock market, it's really not that difficult. Basically, there are many different types of stocks, and many are good for different reasons, and at different times in an economic cycle. It's also important to know that a company's stock can fit into more than one category.

First off are the "cyclical" stocks, so called because if you graph the price of one of these stocks over a long period of time, the graph looks like a roller coaster ride as it matches the ups and down in the overall economy. Companies that have stocks like this (for example, home builders and car manufacturers) are companies that are dependent on good economic times to keep them chugging along.

Then there are, you guessed it, "noncyclical" stocks, that at least in theory do well even in a poor economy because people will continue to buy their products. There is a saying that no matter how bad things get, you still need a bowl of Corn Flakes in the morning. Not surprisingly, then, basic food and beverage makers tend to fall into the noncyclical group.

You've probably heard of "blue-chip" stocks. These are stocks of companies that are well respected, have been around for a long time, and deliver consistent dividends and price growth. Coca-Cola is one of the more blue of the blue chips.

There are also "income" stocks that earn their distinction by paying out healthy dividends to their shareholders. Utilities and banks are good examples of income stocks. Dividends are useful, but if you're a younger investor, dividends are not as important as finding companies that have good growth prospects. As you get older and near retirement, you'll find this steady stream of extra income more valuable.

"Growth" stocks, as you might imagine, are companies that have fast-growing profits. They pay little or no dividends to their shareholders, but they make up for that in

other ways. Because they excel in the business that they're in, their earnings are growing and their price is growing. They're the hot stocks that investors and financial analysts are always talking about.

Measuring the Value of a Stock

Velocity = distance traveled divided by time. Momentum = mass times velocity. Force = mass times acceleration. It's easy to measure the laws of physics that govern the universe. The question is, are there ways to measure the laws that govern the value of a stock in the investment universe? While investing is not an exact science, there are several yardsticks that you can use to help in picking a stock. What you'll find here is just a sample. For a more complete analysis, you should take a look at the companion book in this Clueless series, *If You're Clueless about the Stock Market and Want to Know More*.

- *Price-to-earnings ratio*. One of the best ways to gauge if a stock has a reasonable valuation is to look at the company's earnings and then compare that number with the price of the company's stock. This tool is often called a "P/E" ratio because you have to take the "P" (price per share of the stock) and divide it by the "E" (earnings per share of the stock). You can get earnings information from the company's annual report. You can get the company's price on any given day just by opening up the pages of the *Wall Street Journal, Investor's Business Daily*, or the business section of most large city newspapers, which are at newsstands and at your local library. A company's earnings tells you how profitable the firm is. And if the company shows healthy earnings year after year, that's a good mark in its favor. Also, when you do the math and figure out the P/E ratio, you should compare that number with that of other stocks in its category and to overall market benchmarks like the Dow Jones Industrial Average or the Standard & Poors (S&P) 500 Index. For example, if the stock you like has a P/E of 30, it better have a good reason to be so high, because the P/E for a benchmark like the S&P lately has been around 20. You don't want to pay too much for a stock, and a high P/E tells you the valuation might be unreasonable.

- *Dividend yield*. All you do here is divide the annual dividend (say, $5 per share) by the price per share of the stock (say, $100). The dividend yield in this case would be 5 percent. A solid track record of paying dividends, in both good and bad economic times, is another measure of a company's health. You can get this information from the same sources just given for P/E data. You can also use the dividend yield number to compare the stock to market benchmarks like the S&P, which has been yielding between 2 and 3 percent over the past few years.

- *Price-to-book ratio*. Again, this is jargon for a simple calculation. Book value is just the difference between a company's assets and its liabilities. You can find this information in the annual report. Book value represents what the company would be worth if it were liquidated. Divide the book value by the number of shares of stock (to give you the book value per share) and then take this number and divide it by the current price of the stock. You want the price-to-book ratio to be low. Often a stock is called a bargain because its price is less than the book value. So in a sense you're buying the company for less than it's "worth." Not bad; but often you'll have to settle for a price-to-book ratio that's a little higher.

- *Return on equity*. The annual report should list this figure. It represents the company's net profits after taxes divided by its book value. This data is valuable because it tells you how a company is managing itself. You want this number to be steady year after year. If return on equity is not consistent, that could be a sign of problems, such as an inability to deal with debt.

- *52 weeks hi/low*. This is one of the headings you'll find in the stock tables listed in the business section of your local newspaper or in a national business publication such as the *Wall Street Journal*. This data tells you where the price of your favorite stock has been over the past 52 weeks. It's a good indicator of the stock's price volatility. If the "Hi" number and the "Low" number are really different, it's important to find out what the reason is for the price swings. This data is also a valuable way to tell how much people have been willing to pay for the stock over the past year.

Where to Dig for Stock Information

The annual report of a company is a great place to get most of the vital statistics on the company's value. But don't stop there. Many other resources exist, and some are free. With most of the Internet sites, the way it works is simple: the more basic financial information is provided free of charge so that they can suck you into paying for their more comprehensive services.

- *Value Line Investment Survey*. The mother of all financial data. This source gives you price, earnings, dividend information, and more going back over a decade for thousands of stocks. This book also has expert analysis and historical news. Your best choice for retrieving this tomb is to go to your library; the alternative is to pay over $500. If you have the means, their number is (800) 833-0046.

- The Securities and Exchange Commission (http://www.sec.gov)—Let the government be your one-stop-shopping network for all types of financial data. You can get a company's annual report, with all the information we've just talked about; 10q financial reports, issued for the first three quarters of a company's fiscal year; proxy statements, showing, among other things, how much the company's top executives are paid; and special event reports. The only downside here is that there may be too much information, and it is not always presented in a reader-friendly way. Be prepared to spend some time getting used to the site. When you get to the SEC site, just click on to their EDGAR database.

- Hoover's Inc.(http://www.hoovers.com)—For years this company has put out a remarkable handbook that gives in-depth history and data on hundreds of companies. You can go to your library or bookstore to take a look, but the company also has an online version that's almost as good. Here you can get "Company Capsules" that show your favorite firm's sales, net income, and top competitors, as well as what symbol it trades under and how many employees are on the payroll. This site also has financial news and research material.

- BigCharts (http://www.bigcharts.com)—This site gives you historical charts, quotes, and research on over 34,000 stocks, mutual funds, and indexes. It also shows stocks with the largest percentage gain in price, stocks hitting new 52-week highs and lows, and the most actively traded stocks.

- Microsoft (http://investor.msn.com)—Microsoft lets you track your investments with its "Portfolio manager"; just put in the stock's symbol. It also gives you a running score of how the Dow, Nasdaq, S&P, and 30-year bonds are doing every day. Plus, you can click on to news articles about stocks and investing.

- Quote.com (http://www.quote.com)—A lot of the information you get overlaps from site to site, but the more you look around the more you'll know. Quote.com offers the usual quotes and data, but it also offers an "Industry Watch" service that ties together news, stock prices, and industry indexes for over 100 industries. You can look at how a whole industry is fairing or focus in on the fortunes of an individual company.

- WallSt.com (http://www.wallst.com)—You can use this site to put together a mock portfolio of your favorite stocks and track how they do over time. This site also provides extensive stock reports and up-to-the-minute earnings information.

- PC Quote Inc. (http://www.pcquote.com)—This company is a leading provider of online and real-time stock quotes to financial professionals. Its Web site combines basic stock statistics with the latest headlines in the news that affect stocks.

How to Buy Stocks: The Different Flavors of Brokers

Buying stocks isn't like buying milk at the corner market. For most of the stocks you want to buy, you're going to have to make your purchase through a middleman called a broker. Over the past 20 years there's been a revolution in the brokerage industry that has widened the number of choices you have, but it has also made

things more complicated to understand. Basically, there are three types of firms: full-service brokers, discount brokers, and deep-discount brokers.

Traditional full-service brokers will give you the same extensive range of services they gave your grandparents and great-grandparents. These firms, which include such well-known names as Merrill Lynch and Salomon Smith Barney, will give you a broker who will sit down with you to discuss your goals and risk tolerance. You'll have access to lots of research and educational material. And most important, your full-service broker will keep a vigilant eye on all the key numbers and statistics that we just looked at in the previous section and make recommendations as to what are the good stocks to buy now.

In other words, they do all the dirty work for you. Of course, that comes with a price tag. Full-service brokers charge the most, either by the number of stock trades they make for you or as a percentage of the assets you have with them. They also often require that you keep a large minimum balance with them, maybe $5,000, maybe more. Is it worth it? It depends on how into stock picking you are. I have friends who love doing all the stock homework themselves. It's almost like a sport. And it can be quite addictive. But if you're just starting out with investing, it's best to rely on someone with experience, at least for a while. Once you get acclimated to the logic (and illogic) of the stock market, you can always move to the less expensive discount and deep-discount brokers.

As their names would suggest, what you get from discount brokers is pretty bare-bones. They don't offer as much research information as traditional brokers, and they give little or no investment advice. With the deep-discount variety, you basically get nothing but a way to make trades; you do all the research and keep your own counsel. You'll save money this way, though the prices are always changing as brokerages try to undercut each other. The best way to get the bird's-eye view of who's got what is to look in financial magazines like *Kiplinger's Personal Finance Magazine*, *Money*, and *Smart Money*; every year these publications do stories that rate the top ten in each brokerage category.

Growth versus Value Investing

Knowing what stocks to pick can be really difficult. And there is a wide array of philosophies out there when it comes to choosing securities. The two major schools of thought, growth investing and value investing, both offer impressive track records of market results. They just get there using very different methods.

If you invest using a growth philosophy, the sky's the limit. Going for growth means hitching your wagon to the stocks of well-known, successful companies that have rapidly growing earnings. Earnings is the key for growth players. The company you buy has to be growing faster than the overall market and faster than other companies in its industry. Growth investors also want to see strong sales and return on equity. The price you pay for the stock may be high, but that's okay. If the company has a good earnings growth rate, you can afford to buy high, because the stock should go even higher.

The time to get out of the stock is when the company reports bad earnings. Now it's important to remember that "bad" is a relative term. Even if earnings were up for the current quarter, they may not be up as much as anticipated, and so that's "bad" earnings news. Many a stock has been taken out to the woodshed and shot for committing such sins.

Value investors take the opposite approach. Their craft, also known as fundamental analysis, involves lots of research into the inner workings of a company and its industry. Price is vital to value players, who want to buy companies that are currently selling below their fair market "value." This value is determined by looking at several numbers, including the price-to-earnings ratio and the price-to-book ratio. Value investors are looking for bargains. They also want to make sure the company is in sound financial condition and that management is solid.

You often hear the companies sought after by value investors described as "beaten down" and "ready for a rise." That's because value investing often means buying companies that are considered losers by Wall Street, either because the company has gone through tough financial times or because the industry that the company is in is out of favor. Value investing also requires the patience to ride out a few bad quarters of earning. But if you're a true believer in the value camp, your fundamental analysis

proves that the company is sound; and because you bought the stock so cheap, you're bound to make money when the rest of Wall Street sees what they've been missing.

So which philosophy do you believe in? Of course there's no law that says you have to pick sides. You can choose investments using both strategies to hedge your bets.

Mutual Funds

This is the point in the book where you should start salivating. Mutual funds are an almost perfect investment vehicle for investors who don't have the time, patience, confidence, or instincts to know what stocks to buy, when to buy them, and equally important, when to sell them. With mutual funds, you pay a manager to do all the worrying for you.

Mutual funds are companies that pool together the money of many investors to buy stocks, bonds, or a combination of the two. For a small fee (sometimes not so small), you get a manager to pick your investments for you and to decide when to buy and sell them. The largest mutual funds can have tens of billions of dollars in them, but it didn't used to be that way. In 1960, there were less than 200 mutual funds in the United States; today there are about 7,000 funds.

Mutual funds can be vital to your investment plan for several reasons. First, mutual funds reduce your investment risk somewhat because they usually are buying into hundreds of securities, so you're decreasing the chance that a single bad investment will wipe you out.

Second, you need only a little money to get in. When you buy individual stocks or bonds, you need to buy lots to achieve diversity, and that costs you plenty. But you can start investing in most mutual funds for $1,000, and many will let you in for as little as $50 a month, as long as you follow their rules for making regular contributions. Mutual funds also allow you to reinvest the fund's earnings automatically, which helps your money grow even faster. Be sure to select the automatic reinvestment option when you buy a fund.

Third, these funds have shareholder service departments that you can call up 24 hours

No-Load Stocks: Foreign and Domestic

If you really know what stocks you want to buy and don't want to pay for the services of a broker, you may be in luck. Today, there are hundreds of companies in this country who will sell you their stock directly. And the number of these so-called no-load stocks is growing. Going this route means you'll save on commissions, but it also means you'll have no safety net. You should save this option for when you are mature enough as an investor not to need any financial hand-holding.

That aside, the one big problem with no-load stocks is trying to find which companies offer them. Federal law forbids companies from advertising this opportunity to the world, and you don't see too many stories on no-load stocks in the newspapers. But there are a few books, like *No-Load Stocks*, by Charles Carlson (McGraw-Hill, 1997), and Internet resources (www.netstockdirect.com). Each June, the American Association of Individual Investors (312-280-0170) publishes a list of companies that sell their stock direct to the public ($12.50 for nonmembers). And, of course, once you've done your homework and run the numbers on what companies you want to invest in, you can always just pick up the phone and ask the company's investor relations department point-blank if they have it (they are allowed to tell you if you ask). That's probably the best advice for you anyway, because your decision to buy a stock should not be based on whether or not the stock is no-load.

If you have a yen for the stocks of foreign countries, many firms can accommodate you, with only a slightly different procedure. You'll have to buy so-called ADRs (American depository receipts) for the company through an intermediary. This route still saves you money over going through a broker. Just call the company's investor relations office in the United States for details.

a day, seven days a week, to get all sorts of information about your investments. You also have easy access to your money; you can buy or sell whenever you wish.

There are a couple of fees you may pay for this kind of convenience. A fund's "management fee" is the most basic; that pays the salary of your fund's manager and the other costs of running the fund. Some funds also tack on a "12b-1" fee that pays for the company's marketing and advertising of the fund. And then there are the "loads." There are many versions of this sales charge, ranging from "front-end" loads that come when you first buy shares to "back-end" loads you see when you redeem your shares. There's no reason why you have to pay a load. Most of the best funds are "no-load." And don't be fooled into thinking "the more expensive the fund, the better the fund will be." That may be true for luxury cars and fine wine, but it's certainly not true for mutual funds.

Mutual Funds come in all sorts of flavors, including the following:

- *Aggressive growth*. As the name suggests, these funds don't mind taking big risks with your money in search of big capital gains. They tend to invest in newer, smaller companies whose stocks have high growth potential. They look for quick upward price moves, not high dividends.

- *Growth*. These are not as high-octane as the aggressive growth funds. These funds buy into well-established companies—medium-to-large firms that promise a slow but steady long-term march upward in price.

- *Growth and income*. Healthy dividends are the appeal with these funds. They invest in older, larger businesses that have a history of paying out income consistently. These funds also look for firms that can grow their business and increase the value of their shares.

- *Index*. Instead of trying to beat market benchmarks like the Dow and the S&P 500, index funds just buy all the stocks in the benchmark (for more information on this strategy, see the section in this chapter on indexing).

- *International*. These funds invest in securities of firms outside the United

Diversification

You should never rely on one style of stock investing. And the larger point is that you should never put all your investment money into just stocks, or just bonds, or just mutual funds. You need to spread your money around. The economy affects different types of investments in different ways, so diversification offers the hope that no matter how the economy is doing, at least some of your investments are making you money.

There's a lot of advice out there about what percentage of your investment money should be in stocks, bonds, and mutual funds. One rule is that you should take your age, say 25, out of the number 100. That means in this example that 75 percent of your investment money should be in equities (stocks and stock mutual funds), and the remaining 25 percent should be in bonds and bond mutual funds. As you get older, the amount you put in equities will get smaller and smaller. Whether you buy this theory or not, the basic premise that the younger you are the more aggressive you should be, is valid.

States. Two-thirds of their portfolio must follow this guideline to qualify. Regional international funds stick to a single country or region.

- *Global*. All countries, including the United States, are fair game for this brand of fund. They go wherever they see good growth prospects.

- *Sector*. Sector funds bet on a single industry, say, electronics or health care, to invest in. This ratchets up your risk.

- *Balanced*. Balanced funds try to reduce risk by investing in a portfolio mixed with both stocks and bonds.

How to Make the "Dogs of the Dow" Work for You

Remember, there are many different strategies out there for how to make the most return on your investments. None of these strategies are guaranteed, of course, because past performance is no guarantee of future results. But in his book *Beating the Dow*, Michael O'Higgins (1991) puts forth a relatively simple system, based on serious research, that historically has let investors outperform the stock market.

Here's how it works:

- Take the 30 stocks that make up the Dow Jones Industrial Average and sift out the ten in this group that have the highest dividend yields. Then purchase these companies in equal amounts.

- Every year, run the numbers again to determine the list of the ten highest yielding stocks.

- Sell any of your stocks that fall off the list, and replace them with the new high yielders.

There's also a twist on this system if you're prepared to be a little more risky:

- Take the ten highest yielding of these Dow stocks and narrow down the list even further.

- Pick the five lowest priced stocks out of the ten and buy those five in equal amounts.

- Every year, run the numbers to calculate the five highest

yielding, lowest priced stocks and then readjust your portfolio accordingly.

This strategy has worked in the past for several reasons. First off, this method is often called "Dogs of the Dow" because these high-yielding companies are usually considered the losers in the Dow group. They are out of favor on Wall Street (at least temporarily), which gives you the opportunity to buy the stocks at bargain prices. And because the Dow tends to be made up of strong companies, they usually bounce back, and your money goes along for the ride.

The results are impressive. Investing in the ten highest yielding stocks in this Dow average at the start of each year between 1973 and 1993 produced an annual compounded return of 17.5 percent. And you would have done even better if you had narrowed your stock picking to include only the five lowest priced issues among the ten high yielders; that system paid out a giddy 21.2 percent annual return. If you had invested in all 30 of the Dow stocks over the same period of time, you would have returned 11.2 percent annually.

For more details you can always go to your library or to the bookstore to pick up a copy of this very helpful publication.

- *Corporate bond*. These bond funds seek high income by purchasing the bonds of corporations. You usually see them in two categories: high-yield and investment-grade. Also called "junk bonds," high-yield bonds get that moniker because along with greater yield, investors bear a greater risk of default. The investment-grade variety is a safer, though less profitable, option.

- *U.S. government bond*. This is as safe as mutual funds get. These funds buy securities from the U.S. Treasury, which are backed by the full faith and credit of Uncle Sam. Added risk can occur if they supplement their portfolio with debt issued by federal agencies.

International Investing

You really should consider having at least a little global exposure, not only because of the basic theory of diversification but because of all the great buying opportunities abroad. There are so many changes going on around the world now: markets are opening up in Eastern Europe and in other former Communist countries, Latin America is shedding its protectionism and statism, and the Pacific Rim promises growth opportunities (along with a bumpy ride). Just remember that the normal disclaimer about risk also applies here. Moreover, you usually have the added bonus of worrying about fluctuations in the various countries' currencies bringing down the value of your investments.

You can stake your claim in the world of international investing through stocks, bonds, and mutual funds. Your broker can help you decide how much exposure you should have abroad, what foreign stocks and bonds look good, and also what countries and regions have the most potential. Good ways to go global with mutual funds include finding ones that invest in an index of one or more foreign countries (much like the Dow or S&P 500 is an index of U.S. stocks), or in a basket of many companies from many countries.

There are quite a few fund managers with decades of international stock-picking experience under their belt who can handle your money. Financial publications like *Kiplinger's*, *Money*, and *Smart Money* often do stories about the best international fund managers. Still another way to get international exposure is to buy stocks of U.S. companies that do a large amount of their business overseas.

- *Mortgage securities*. These funds buy mortgage-backed securities from agencies with funny-sounding names like Ginnie Mae.

- *Global bond*. Like global stock funds, these funds travel the globe for the best deals.

How do you know which funds fall into what categories? When you initially call a fund to get their investment literature, they'll send you a prospectus that should (at least in theory) spell out what strategy the fund uses to make money. I say "in theory" because the average prospectus is so vague and written in such dense legalize that even seasoned investors have a hard time figuring them out.

As an added bonus, mutual fund companies will sometimes say their fund is in one category when in fact the fund is buying into the type of investments that should put it in an entirely different category. Some funds do this so they can tell you they out-performed all the funds in their category (which sounds great until you realize that they don't belong in that category). And don't count on the government to step in and correct matters; federal rules on fund classification are pretty porous. When you call to get your fund prospectus, also ask for an annual report. That will give you a specific breakdown of what the fund invests in.

Luckily, you need go only as far as your library or newsstand to get solid information on mutual funds. The personal finance magazines listed previously in the chapter are all good to flip through. In addition, *Mutual Funds* magazine can be valuable since funds are its specialty. On top of their monthly mutual fund reviews, many publica-tions also publish annuals that list extensive data and rankings on thousands of funds. This will give you a bird's-eye view of what funds are out there and who's a cut above the rest.

As you do your research, you should look for mutual funds that display certain qual-ities. Information on individual funds can be found in the prospectus and other lit-erature you'll get from the fund when you call; comparative information can be found by reviewing the many personal finance publications. Here are some impor-tant points to consider when you're doing your research:

Pros and Cons of Dollar-Cost Averaging

One of the first bits of investment advice you're likely to hear when you tell friends, family, and "financial experts" that you're going to buy stocks or mutual funds is "be sure to buy them using dollar-cost averaging." This odd-sounding strategy is relatively simple to understand, actually. All it means is that you invest your money in fixed amounts at regular intervals, as opposed to dumping all your money in at once. This strategy takes advantage of the ever-present fluctuations in the markets. Because the amount you invest remains constant, you buy more shares when the price is low and fewer shares when the price is high.

But it is wrong to think that this is always the best strategy. In many cases it's not. For example, in a market that is constantly rising, you're better off investing your money in one lump sum and then watching as your shares rise along with the stock's price. If you use dollar-cost averaging (say, on a monthly basis) in a rising market, it'll cost you money because you end up paying more each month for fewer shares.

Dollar-cost averaging is a winning plan when the market is declining or is fluctuating. In a declining market, steady periodic investments allow you to buy more shares at increasingly lower prices. And during fluctuations, dollar-cost averaging lets you smooth out the ride and reduce the risk.

It all depends on your risk tolerance. If you put all your money in at once, there is a risk that you'll be "buying at the top," and you'll end up in bad shape if the stock's price then goes south. Dollar-cost averaging is the safer route.

	Monthly Investment	Share Price	How Many Shares
Market Going Up	$200, $200, $200	$5, $8, $10	40, 25, 20
Market Going Down	$200, $200, $200	$10, $8, $5	20, 25, 40
Choppy Market	$200, $200 $200, $200	$10, $8, $5 $10	20, 25, 40 20

- *Style to fit your goals and risk tolerance.* Some funds are good for different reasons. If you have a long time horizon, then maybe you can afford the risk of a more aggressive fund. Or if your risk tolerance is low, you should consider sticking with funds that pick blue-chip stocks and/or investment-grade bonds. Remember to diversify your fund purchases; some should be more aggressive than others. Also, you can buy into some mutual funds that practice the "value" philosophy of investing and others that use the "growth" method.

- *Performance.* Don't just look at how a fund has done in the past year. You need to see a long-term record of three, five, and hopefully more years. Along with a consistently strong long-term record, the fund should also score high in its particular investment category, such as aggressive growth, global bond, and so on.

- *Risk and fees.* Check the volatility rankings in the personal finance magazines for the funds you are considering. Also, look at the prospectus for all the different fees they tack on.

Another great source for general background information on mutual funds is the Investment Company Institute (ICI), which is the national association of the investment company industry (www.ici.org). The Institute's members represent more than 63 mil-

Personal Finance Information on the Web?

It seems there are more free tolls on the Internet to help you with your personal finances than there are stars in the sky. Most of the sites listed here have free areas and pay areas. The usual trade-off is free information provided as a loss leader to get you interested in other pay products.

A good starting point is the site run by CNBC, the cable personal finance network (http://www.cnbc.com). They offer lots of investing information, as well as links to other financial Web sites. Their "investment tool kit" gives you live stock market data, business news, and financial information. With links to information from MSNBC, CNBC, and Microsoft Investor, it's an easy way to stay abreast of the changing economic environment. They also have historical charts, company news, an investment risk test, an asset allocator, an income tax estimator, and a cash flow worksheet.

Money Advisor (http://www.moneyadvisor.com) gives you myriad interactive calculators for your investment, mortgage, and insurance needs. You also get links to the Web sites of government agencies and financial institutions.

The three main stock markets also have useful sites. The American Stock Exchange (http://www.amex.com), the New York Stock Exchange (http://www.nyse.com), and Nasdaq (http://www. nasdaq.com) provide market information, charts, and educational material.

A good comprehensive site to go to for information on bonds and the world of fixed-income investments is http://www.investinginbond.com.

Most major mutual fund companies also have Web sites. Two of the giants, Fidelity and Vanguard, are especially noteworthy. Fidelity (http://www.fid-inv.com) will show you how the growth of your investments can be affected by factors like inflation, taxes, and varying rates of return. Vanguard (http://www.vanguard.com) offers short pieces of investment advice, as well as a very educational 20-question mutual fund quiz.

You can keep track of the ever-changing tax rules by visiting the site of the Internal Revenue Service (HYPERLINK http://www.irs.ustreas.gov). This site serves up statistics and tax information, including all the forms and publications you need to fill out your taxes.

Have you ever wanted to see how many Pakistani rupees or Greek drachmas equal one American dollar? Let the Universal Currency Converter (http://www.xe.net/currency/) show you the way. It allows you to perform interactive foreign exchange rate conversions on the Net.

And if you're thinking of starting a company, you can even download a mock business plan from Palo Alto Software (pasware.com/sample.htm).

lion individual shareholders and manage more than \$4.8 trillion. While you're trolling around this site, be sure to click yourself a copy of ICI's "Mutual Fund Fact Book."

The Power of Indexing

One type of mutual fund is an "index" mutual fund. These funds operate under the philosophy "if you can't beat 'em, join 'em." Instead of trying to pick which stocks or bonds are going to do best at any given time, these funds simply buy into the investments of market benchmarks. There are many benchmarks, ranging from the Standard & Poor's 500 Index (which is made up of 500 large, well-known U.S. stocks) to the Wilshire 5000 Index (which includes just about every large, medium, and small stock you can think of). So in the case of a fund that indexes the S&P 500, all your fund does is to buy those 500 stocks. It's that simple.

There are many advantages to this style of investing. It's a good choice for beginning investors who are still unsure of the markets but are prepared to face the risks and rewards of holding mutual funds. Also, this really is autopilot investing. With many other mutual funds, you have to worry that if your Merlin-like fund manager retires or leaves to start up his own firm, your money will be stuck with one of his apprentices. With index funds, the manager isn't coming up with any ideas of what stocks to buy, he's just buying stocks on a list. You also usually get diversification with index funds, and there really is safety in numbers.

Low cost is a key reason to go with indexes. You don't pay as high a management fee since your manager doesn't have to do as much work. Finally, index funds save money because it would cost you too much to do this style of investing on your own. Just think how much you'd have to pay your broker to buy 5,000 different stocks.

The disadvantage to indexing is pretty straightforward: You can't expect too many stellar years. To use a baseball analogy, you're not swinging for the fences with index funds, so you won't hit home runs. But you won't strike out, either. Basically what you're settling for is singles and a few doubles. Also, not all indexes give you diversity (such as those that mimic the stocks of a single foreign nation like Mexico), and many don't do as well as the all-famous S&P 500.

There are over 100 index funds, and they come in all different shapes and sizes. There are stock indexes that track large companies, medium companies, small companies, technology companies, and several foreign countries in a particular region. And there are foreign and domestic bond indexes that cover various maturities and investment grades.

The index that gets mimicked the most is the S&P 500. And with good reason; it has a remarkable record over the past 20 years. The companies that make up the index read like a *Who's Who* list of corporate America. About two dozen mutual funds currently offer their version of the S&P 500 index; Vanguard, based in Valley Forge, Pennsylvania, has been at it the longest.

Bonds

A bond is an IOU, a promise made by a corporation or by your government to pay you back for whatever amount of money you choose to lend them. Not only do they pledge to pay you back what you lent them (which is called the principal), they also reward your generosity by paying you a rate of interest at scheduled intervals.

Historically, bonds have returned far less than stocks, though bonds offer some safety as well as a certain yield. As you get older, investments like bonds that offer a steady income will look more and more appealing. But if you're younger, bonds should occupy only a small portion of your investment portfolio. If you're in your twenties, for example, you can afford to be a little aggressive. Your concern should be the high capital appreciation that can be found in stocks and stock mutual funds.

Bonds will always fill a niche in your financial plan, however, so you should be aware of the forces that affect them. First you have to look at how interest rates influence bonds. When interest rates rise, bond prices drop, and when interest rates drop, bond prices rise.

Second, you have to understand the risk-reward relationship of how credit ratings affect bonds. There are several agencies that rate the default risk, or the safety, of the bonds that are out there. As you might expect, ratings of "AAA" are good—and as the grades get lower, that indicates an increasing lack of confidence that the issuer of the bond will be able to pay interest and principal. As a rule, the lower the bond's grade, the higher the bond will yield. It's pretty simple to understand why: The higher yield compensates you for the risk that your bond will default and you will lose everything.

Like stocks, there are many different types of bonds; some are riskier than others and some are more profitable than others. There are "U.S. government securities" that are issued or backed by Uncle Sam. They offer safety from default, but not from loss of value.

Then there are "corporate bonds," which are issued by private industry. These IOUs vary in credit rating from AAA to B and below. Bonds in the B range are often called "junk bonds" by detractors because of their risk; they are called "high-yield" bonds by their advocates because they reward investors for that risk.

Next come "municipal bonds," which are issued by state and local governments. These bonds are floated to pay for roads, bridges, and even baseball stadiums. These IOUs are unique in that the income they pay you is free from federal income tax and, in some cases, exempt from state and local taxes as well.

And finally, there are "foreign bonds," which are issued by corporations and governments in foreign lands. They may offer great opportunities for profits, but they carry the risks of political and economic upheaval, default, and the special risks associated with currency fluctuation that we talked about earlier.

As with stocks, the best way for novice investors to get into bonds is through mutual funds. Let a fund manager do all the dirty work. All you have to do is pick which categories of bond funds you want to invest in, which is based on the categories of bonds we've just discussed.

How Investing Affects Your Taxes

Your biggest tax bite from investing will come when you sell part or all of your investments. But even if you don't touch your investments, the IRS still wants its due every April 15.

When you sell your investments for a profit (which is called a "capital gain"), how long you held them for will determine how much of the gain will be gobbled up in taxes. The government likes to promote buy-and-hold investing, so it penalizes investors when they sell too quickly. This breaks down to different taxes for your long-term capital gains (investments held for more than 18 months), short-term capital gains (investments held for a year or less), and so-called mid-term gains (investments held for dates in between). The maximum tax on short-term gains is currently whatever your income tax rate is. For long-term gains, the maximum is 20 percent of the gain, and for mid-termers, the max is 28 percent.

To calculate how much your capital gain is, you first have to calculate your investment's "basis." On your purchases of stocks, bonds, and mutual funds, the basis begins as whatever you paid for the investment, including commissions and other fees.

Even if you don't sell any of your investments, there are other taxes. With stocks, you are taxed every year on the dividends that you earn. With corporate bonds, you're taxed on interest payments. With U.S. Treasury securities, there's no state or local tax on interest. And for municipal bonds, there's no federal tax on interest.

With mutual funds, the interest and dividends you earn are taxed every year, even if you never see the loot because you automatically reinvested them into the fund. Also, the basis when you sell shares in a mutual fund can be tricky. You may have to choose between the average basis method, the first in/first out method, or the specific identification method to do your calculations. Luckily, most mutual funds do your basis homework for you (and send you the data along with other tax information when you sell), so you don't have to bother.

Because federal tax rules fall under the whim of Congress, the information given here may change next year or the year after that. Or it may stay the same. That's why so many people end up seeking professional help in filling out their tax forms every year.

Alternative Investments Like Gold, Art, and Collectibles

When your grandfather was a young man, gold was considered a valuable part of any investment portfolio. Gold promised to be a useful hedge against inflation and economic turmoil. Today there is no compelling reason to put any of your cash into gold. Times have changed and the gold industry has changed.

But if you still want a little sparkle in your financial plan, there are several ways to get into gold. You can buy gold coins from the U.S. government and from other countries. You can buy stock in companies that mine and process gold. And you can invest in mutual funds that primarily hold gold stocks.

There's a wonderful show on PBS where people bring in their family heirlooms and other antiques, and appraisers wax poetic about how historically valuable great-grandma's andiron is. Then, with the owner grinning from ear to ear, the appraiser says the asking price for the antique has increased ten-fold. It's fun to watch if you're really bored. But it's important to remember that these people are the exception. Most of

the stuff you have up in your attic and most of the stuff that you might consider buying, are not going to give you a lot of value for the dollar.

The only reason to buy art and other collectibles is for personal enjoyment, not profit. Occasionally, there are price run-ups on certain collectibles. If that happens for you, great. Usually, however, these are short-term bubbles that quickly pop, leaving the gullible with a big hole in their wallets. So don't make bets on art and collectibles; it's as foolish as buying lottery tickets.

Real Estate

In the recent past, real estate was considered a valuable investment. During the 1970s housing prices soared as the Baby Boomers emerged from college, got married, and went looking for a home with a white picket fence. Because demand for housing went up, so did housing prices. You could buy a house, do a few improvements, quickly sell, and make big bucks. Guess what? The party's over.

Today, housing prices in your area may still beat inflation, but not like they used to. Times have changed and the supply and demand issues are not the same. Of course, this is not to say that you shouldn't buy a home. Far from it. That call is up to you. But you should view your house as a home, not a get-rich-quick investment.

There are still good reasons to stop renting an apartment to buy a home. Top on this list are the tax breaks that Uncle Sam gives you. The government has long had a policy of encouraging home ownership. And to this end, it allows you to deduct from your taxes the interest you pay when you borrow to buy a home. In addition, as mentioned in chapter 2, 1998 marks the first full year that there is no capital gains tax on the first $500,000 in profits when you sell your home.

If you're tempted to use this opportunity to buy a home, you can enlist the help of a mortgage reporting service to find low loan rates in your area. On the Web, HSH Associates (http://www.hsh.com) and Mortgage Marketing Information Services (http://www.interest.com) both offer free listings of lenders and what they offer. You can also do comparison shopping by calling up lenders found under the "Mortgage" listings in your Yellow Pages.

Check Out Your Financial Adviser

Before you hand your life's savings over to a broker or financial planner, you should do a little bit of investigative reporting.

One good starting point is to call the Financial Adviser Alert, which is run by the National Council of Individual Investors and the National Fraud Exchange (800-822-0416). They examine the records of the Federal Deposit Insurance Corporation, the Securities and Exchange Commission, the Department of Justice, and other federal agencies, state commissions on securities, and self-regulatory groups like the National Association of Securities Dealers (NASD). They'll be able to tell you if your broker or financial adviser has been subject to criminal or civil actions.

A useful way to check your broker's record is to look up her CRD report (which stands for Central Registration Depository). The NASD will give you this information if you call them (800-289-9999) or write to them at: Public Disclosure, NASD Regulation, Inc., P.O. Box 9401, Gaithersburg, MD 20898-9401. Or you can check their Web site (http://www.nasdr.com).

If you're having problems with a financial planner, you may want to contact one of the appropriate organizations:

Certified Financial Planner Board of Standards, 1660 Lincoln St., Suite 3050, Denver, CO 80264-3001, (800) CFP-MARK.

Chartered Financial Consultants, The American College, 270 Bryn Mawr Ave., Bryn Mawr, PA 19010, (215) 526-1000.

You might want to consider paying for the services of a mortgage broker. These people act as intermediaries to hook up home buyers with lenders. One benefit of this service is that brokers may be able to shop nationally for a cheaper rate or get a slightly lower rate from a lender they deal with frequently. Another plus is that brokers may get you a cheaper "wholesale" rate through a bank than you'd get if you went on your own through a lender's retail account.

Mortgage brokers don't lend and can't approve loans. While anyone can use a mortgage broker, keep in mind that the fee for this service comes in extra loan points (a point is 1 percent of the mortgage amount) or in a higher rate. How much you'll pay varies greatly, but paying one point in compensation (or $1,000 on a $100,000 loan) is not unusual.

This service might be best if you need assistance from a mortgage broker to help you qualify for a loan because of a black mark on your credit record or because you're self-employed. The National Association of Mortgage Brokers has over 30 affiliates nationwide that can help you find brokers in your area. Brokers can be checked through your state's licensing commission.

YOUR college Investments

CHAPTER FOUR

When the time comes that your kids need money for college, how much of it will be left for school if the IRS, inflation, or the vicissitudes of the stock market eat it up?

There are some new ways to save for college that minimize these risks. There are also many traditional options that have been around for years. If the college planning that's going on is for you and not your children, there's a separate list of questions you have to ask yourself.

When Should You Start Planning for College?

The answer is simple: a lot sooner than you think. If you've just gotten out of school and are starting your first job, financing your yet-to-be-born child's education may seem a little bizarre. But if you're married and are thinking about having kids, now is the time to

Teach Your Kids the Value of Saving and Investing

One way to make sure you'll have enough money to pay the college bills is to have kids who act responsibly with money. Easier said than done? Sure, but that's what parenting is all about.

On the savings side, you can do several things. When you dole out your child's allowance, you can reach an understanding that part of it will go into her own savings. You can take your child to the bank to open her own savings account. Then, using the account statements, you can graph for her how her money is growing each month.

On the investing side, you also have options. While it's not a sound idea to have your child play the markets with real money, there's something to be said for exposing children to the concepts of risk and reward that you find with investing. And there's a relatively safe way to do it. Give your kids play money to "invest" in stocks that they can track in the business section of your local newspaper. When the stocks go up over time, give them a proportional bonus on their regular allowance. If the stocks they pick decline, take a small percentage out of their allowance. After this goes on for a while you may be amazed at what savvy stock pickers your kids can be. And all in the name of extra candy money!

do some homework to find out about the many ways to pay those future university bills.

The reason you have to start this early is that college costs have been skyrocketing for more than a generation. Over the last 20 years, college tuition has ballooned by 400 percent, from $2,577 in 1976 to over $10,500 today. And that's not even the total bill. College costs can also include room and board, transportation, books and supplies, and all the "other" expenses. At a private college, that can mean a bill of over $20,000 a year.

Historically, the rate of college costs has been increasing by 7 percent to 12 percent annually. More recently, however, it has slowed to 6 percent. The problem is, that's still twice the rate of inflation. And even at 6 percent, if you project what costs will be in 20 years (when junior gets to college), it comes out to $65,000 a year for private school and $31,000 for public school.

But so far the benefits of a college degree still outweigh the costs. The President's Council of Economic Advisers estimates that the return on your investment of earning a university diploma is quite high: between 11 and 13 percent a year for life. As we saw in chapter 3, that's good value for the dollar.

College is more and more a prerequisite for success, not simply a bonus. Ten years ago, less than half the nation's high school graduates enrolled in college. By 1996, two-thirds were college bound. According to the U.S. Census Bureau, the median income for people with only a high school education is $19,547. If you have a bachelor's degree, that median income jumps to $31,569. And if you go for a master's degree, that number bumps up to $40,586. Knowledge is not only liberty, it can also be money in the bank.

If you start early, you'll be able to manage the costs so they don't overwhelm you. In the same way that time is on your side when it comes to financing goals like retirement, time is your best friend when you're financing college. If you wait too long, though, you'll be forced to be too aggressive with your investment plan.

Two College Scenarios: Paying for Your Child versus Paying for Yourself

It really comes down to a question of long-term versus short-term planning. If we're talking about your child, then the picture is pretty clear. You know it's worth it to make the financial sacrifices. As we've just seen, college is a good return on your investment. So that means you'll need to start investing early, which we'll get to shortly in this chapter. You'll also need to look into government and private financial aid, loans, scholarships—the works. Since your plans probably call for sending your pride and joy to a four-year university, full-time, we will look at how to deal with all of these issues and where to go for help.

But if you're the one who's contemplating a return to college to get a higher degree or to change professions, the rules are a little different. You need to think about several issues. First off, if you're thinking about going back to school in just a year or two, your long-term investment strategy is out the window. You won't be able to be aggressive with your money, because you need the money now.

You first need to sit down and do a cost-benefit analysis. Is it really worth it to get a higher degree? How much could your salary increase with an M.S., M.B.A., or Ph.D.? We saw what the averages are, but the number for you will vary from profession to profession. Some fields value a graduate degree more than others do.

You also need to think about whether you can afford to go back to school full-time or if a part-time strategy makes more sense. It's possible your employer will help you pay for the extra education if the company thinks it will make you a more valuable asset in the firm. We will explore the use of extra education for career advancing or career jumping, as well as how to get there, in the later part of this chapter.

Investing to Help Pay the College Bills

College tuition is a big expense, so you should plan on several different strategies to help pay the bills. Investing is just one of those strategies, but if you start early enough, it can take care of much of the expense. The easiest way to get started is to set aside a small portion of your salary each month to contribute to your child's college fund. It might surprise you how even a little money can grow over time.

For example, to accumulate $10,000 over an 18-year period, how much do you think you would need to invest each month? Assuming a 10 percent earnings rate (which is about what the historic return is for stocks and stock mutual funds), you would need to contribute only $17 each month. That's less than your cable bill. That's less than your phone bill. That's less than a large pizza and drinks delivered to your door. But if you wait until there is only five years to go before college, you will need to put in $151 a month to get the same results.

How much risk should you take with your investments? There are two answers: How much time do you have? And what's your risk tolerance? If you have 18 years to work with, many financial experts agree that you can be aggressive. You can consider a college fund that is 100 percent in stocks and stock mutual funds. As your child enters junior high, however, you need to cut back on this aggressiveness and shift your investments so that 20 to 30 percent is in bonds and bond mutual funds. And when your child is from ages 14 to 18, an asset mix of 40 percent stock investments, 40 percent bond investments, and 20 percent cash investments (such as CDs and money market funds) is prudent. This strategy reduces the risk that a sudden stock market drop will greatly set back your financial plan.

Of course, you should take only as much risk as you are comfortable with. For example, have you never invested in stocks or bonds, or have you been in these markets for more than five years? Your experience level is important. Are you comfortable with investments that may lose money from time to time, as long as the investment offers the potential for high long-term results? You really need to do a gut check. For example, many aggressive growth mutual funds (which you saw described in chapter 3) have been known to drop 20 percent or more in value during brief periods. Are you the kind of person who will quickly sell, instead of being patient and letting the fund make a comeback? You may want to go back to chapter 3 for a more complete exploration of the various ways to invest your money, as well as an explanation of the many risks and rewards.

Who Should Control the Investments?

There are several ways to set up your child's college fund. Each has advantages and disadvantages with regards to taxes, financial aid issues, and plain old control. The obvious route is just to put the account in your name, not your child's name. That ensures that you have control over how the money is eventually spent. It also means that when it comes time to fill out financial aid forms (which we will get to next in this chapter) you'll have the pleasant surprise to know that only a small portion of the parents' assets are subject to financial aid contribution requirements. But the disadvantages are that the money will get taxed at your tax rate, not your child's, which is probably a lot lower than yours.

A second option is to save under your child's name. For example, you can go to a

bank, broker, or mutual fund and set up a UGMA (which stands for Uniform Gifts to Minors Act) custodial account that lets you invest in securities like mutual funds in your child's name. Another such account, UTMA (Uniform Transfers to Minors Act), lets the child own any type of property.

The upside to this strategy is that the investments are dealt only child-sized taxes. For children under age 14, the first $650 of interest, dividends, or capital gains (unearned income) is free from federal tax, and the next $650 is taxed at only 15 percent. After that, the unearned income is taxed at the parent's marginal rate. For kids over 14, the first unearned $650 is tax-free like before, but the next $24,000 is taxed at 15 percent. This is quite a break.

The downside with this type of account is twofold. First, the money you stash away in this account is not yours anymore. You cannot use the money later for your needs; and when your child reaches "adulthood," which can mean age 18 to 25 depending on what state you live in, he can spend the dough however he pleases, whether that be college or a shiny new Mustang. The other problem is that a large part of your child's assets count against you when you're applying for financial aid.

Financial Aid Information: An Introduction

Financial aid comes from several sources. The federal government, which has a long-standing policy of encouraging kids to go to college, offers a wide range of aid. Your state, too, gives out assistance. And universities also offer separate, and sometimes more specialized, aid.

The kind of aid you get will vary. You may get a grant, which is basically free money. Some of the more well-known grants are federal. The Pell grant is designed for low-income families, and the gift ranges from a few hundred dollars to around $3,000 a year. The average recipient last year got a little over $1,500. How much you get depends on how needy you are, how expensive the school is, and whether your child will attend full-time or part-time.

Other grants include the SEOG (Supplemental Educational Opportunity Grant) federal program, which goes to those with the greatest need. The money comes from

Uncle Sam, but it is funneled to schools, who then decide who gets how much. And how much can be as high as $4,000, though grants of around $1,500 are considered very good. There are also state grants that are doled out on the basis of need and academic ability. You'll need to call the Department of Education or Education Commission in that state to find out what's available. Of course, you'll have to meet their specific residency requirements to qualify.

Then there are the many types of loan plans to help you bridge the gap between what you can pay and what you'll end up having to pay. First off is the Perkins federal loan program, which colleges offer to students based on need. Undergraduates can borrow up to $3,000 a year, to a maximum of $15,000. The interest rate for payback is only 5 percent, and repayment doesn't have to begin until nine months after graduation. The average for such a loan was more than $1,200 for the 1995–96 academic year.

Then there are two kinds of Stafford loans, subsidized and unsubsidized. The subsidized Staffords are need-based, and Uncle Sam helps you out by paying the interest on the loans while the student is in school. Repayment of the interest and principal of the loan is then deferred until six months after graduation. The average subsidized Stafford loan was almost $3,500.

The unsubsidized variety differs in that financial need is not a consideration to qualify. With these Stafford loans interest starts accruing from day one, but students can defer payments of principal until six months after getting the diploma.

Another type of loan is the PLUS (Parents' Loans for Undergraduate Students) loan. Parents can use this to pay whatever college bills are left after financial aid is awarded. The low interest rate is adjusted each year, with a cap of 9 percent. Interest begins accruing immediately. Repayment begins after two months. Parents flocked to this option last year, taking out, on average, $5,800 in PLUS loans.

The Ins and Outs of the FAFSA and Other Financial Aid Forms

The first step to find out what grants and loans you're eligible for is to fill out the Free Application for Federal Student Aid (FAFSA). You can get a copy at public libraries, college financial aid offices, and high schools. The form is required if you want to get federal assistance, and it's usually also required by the colleges. It's a very nosy form, asking questions like how much did you make last year and how much is in your checking and savings accounts. Once the numbers of your finances are crunched, you get back in the mail a Student Aid Report (SAR) that tells you what your expected family contribution (or EFC) is.

The EFC is the key to how much you're going to have to shell out for college bills. That's because your financial aid eligibility is calculated by taking the total cost of the college in question (say, $10,000) and subtracting from that the expected family contribution (say, $7,000). The gap between the college cost and your EFC (in this case $3,000) is how much you may get in aid.

Individual colleges have their own definition of what your expected contribution should be. That's why many make you fill out another form, called the CSS (College Scholarship Service) profile. This form asks many of the same nosy questions to determine how needy you are; and you can get the form from the same places that keep the FAFSA. But this form is less generous than the FAFSA, and it differs from the federal form in several areas. First, the CSS profile asks you to include home equity in the EFC formula. That can be bad news if you've built up a lot of equity. The profile also expects a minimum student contribution, usually from savings and student jobs.

And just when you thought all the paperwork was done, remember that some schools require a second financial aid form to determine your eligibility for specialized scholarships and grants, such as those based on your religious affiliation or intended major.

Where to Go for Financial Aid Information and Advice

There are lots of resources out there for you. A trip to the library or bookstore can yield plenty of solid information.

- *College Financial Aid for Dummies*, by Dr. Herm Davis and Joyce Lain Kennedy (IDG Books Worldwide), includes copies of the FAFSA and other financial aid forms, with detailed line-by-line explanations and advice. This book is also loaded down with addresses and college stats.

- *Financing College*, by Kristin Davis (Kiplinger Books, 1996) offers more comprehensive investment and money management advice. The book is also valuable for anyone looking for data on scholarships and how to calculate financial need.

- *Don't Miss Out: The Ambitious Student's Guide to Financial Aid*, by Robert and Anna Leider (Octameron Press, annual). You'll find myriad financial aid tips, as well as a complete breakdown of the aid process.

- *Kaplan You Can Afford College*, by Kaplan (Simon & Schuster, 1997).

There are also many financial planners who would love to give you advice (for just a small fee). They may go by the name "financial aid adviser" or some other title, but there's no license or other certification to prove that the aid adviser is for real. You'll need to find out what qualifications they have and do a background check on them, just as you would for any other financial planner (see chapter 3 for information on how to inspect credentials).

Where to Go for Scholarships

Scholarships are just another part of your overall strategy for financing college—along with investing, loans, and grants. It's just a piece of the puzzle, but it can be a juicy piece. It's also a part of the process that your child can (and should) be actively involved in.

There are thousands upon thousands of scholarships. Some are open to everyone, others are narrowed based on grade-point average, hobbies, religion, speaking skills, or the ability to throw a wicked curve ball.

Step one is to go to your local library; there are plenty of books on finding scholarships. Step two is to go to the high school guidance counselor, who should be loaded up with such documents. Next, check out your employer, as well as professional organizations.

The Internet is also a valuable resource. A good first step is to go on to the Scholarship Page (http://www.iwc.pair.com/scholarshipage). There you can just click on to links to all the major scholarship sites.

One site is fastWEB (http://www.studentservices.com/fastweb). You will have to fill out a detailed list of personal information to get a search that will match your child's specific skills and interests to a database of over 275,000 scholarships. It's wise to keep your profile intentionally vague so that you'll get as many hits as possible.

CollegeNet (http://www.collegenet.com) is another site where you'll have to fill out all sorts of personal data. But it's the best way to narrow down what scholarships can work for you.

FreSch: The Free Scholarship Search Service (http://www.freschinfo.com) provides tips on finding and applying for scholarships, a FAQ section (frequently asked questions), and links to other sites.

Also, don't think in terms of your child winning "The Scholarship." It's important to apply to as many scholarships as possible because (1) you never really know what awards your child is going to win, and (2) it's foolish to think that any one scholarship is going to pay off in a big way. Rather, your strategy should be to go after a lot of little scholarships. A hundred dollars here, a hundred dollars there—it suddenly starts adding up to real money.

It's also profitable to check out what scholarships might be available from service organizations that your child or your family belongs to. You never know unless you try.

Internet Resources

Make sure you're sitting in a comfortable chair when you're surfing the Net for financial aid information and advice. There's just so much out there, it's hard to know where to start. Listed here are just the beginnings of what's helpful on the Web.

- The U.S. Department of Education's site (http://www.ed.gov/offices/ope/) has education news, an electronic version of the FAFSA form, links to colleges and educational resources, and extensive financial aid advice.

- The College Board has a site (http://www.collegeboard.org) that has financial aid information, an online essay evaluation, and answers to frequently asked questions.

- *U.S. News and World Report* (http://www.usnews.com/edu) has more college info on the Web than in their magazine. They offer rankings for 1,400 colleges and universities; they let you find your "ideal" school; and they have an admissions calendar.

- *Chronicle of Higher Education* is another well-respected print resource with an Internet site (http://www.chronicle.merit.edu). They provide helpful stories to keep you up to date with college issues as well as news of finance and personal planning for college.

- Peterson's.com (http://www.petersons.com) is the educational information center. If you click onto their

(continued)

Prepaid College Tuition Plans: A New Trend

Prepaid plans are very popular in the states that have them. Each state has slightly different rules, but the basic concept is pretty simple to understand. It works like this: If you're worried about skyrocketing college costs, prepaid plans let you lock in tomorrow's education costs using today's prices. If you want to, you can start paying for your child's university years today, even if college is 18 years away.

With most states you can either pay all the tuition up front, or in monthly installments. That gives you flexibility. But it also gives you the option of, say, taking the money you've already aggressively invested for your child and plunking it into a prepaid plan in the last few years before college as a way of throttling back on your risk, as we discussed earlier in this chapter. The one downside to that strategy is that when your expected family contribution is calculated for financial aid purposes, these prepaid plans lower the cost of college and therefore lower the amount of aid you can qualify for.

The advantage of prepaid tuition plans is that they're a hedge against the possibility that college inflation will continue to outpace regular inflation, as well as the return you could get from many types of investments. If you think college prices will rise at a 10 percent annual clip (as they have in some past years), why not lock the prices in now? After all, you'll save yourself the trouble of trying to grow your money fast enough to pay the bills.

The disadvantage is that if college inflation rises only at 5 to 6 percent annually (as is the recent trend), then you're probably better off investing the money with mutual funds. As we saw in chapter 3, if you start early and contribute often to stock and/or stock mutual funds, there is great potential for growing your child's college kitty.

Also, what if your child ends up not going to college? With many of the state plans, you're out of luck; you'll get back what you put in, but without any of the interest it accumulated. So after inflation, you're basically losing money on the deal.

It's also important to consider the tax status of college prepaid plans. Contributions made to these plans enjoy tax-deferred treatment, so you'll pay taxes only at the time of distribution. If the distribution happens when your child starts paying tuition, the tax will only cover the gain in value between how much you put into the plan and how much it is worth at distribution. And the tax will be payable at the student's tax rate, not the parent's rate. If the distribution is made as a refund, the tax on the gain will be payable at the tax rate of the recipient of the refund.

What Prepaid Plans Are Out There?

Right now almost 20 states are offering one version or another of these plans, but that number is constantly changing. Several states, such as South Carolina and Washington, open up to the public beginning in the 1998–99 school year. Oregon's prepaid tuition plan is scheduled to come online in the year 2000. And a few states, like Michigan and Wyoming, are not currently open to new customers.

Each plan has its own variation on the prepaid theme, but in Virginia it works like this: The Virginia Prepaid Education Program (or VPEP) pays full in-state tuition and fees at any public college or university in Virginia. This includes the state's

"Public Ivy" schools, such as James Madison University and the University of Virginia. The benefits can also be used toward covering tuition and fees at Virginia's private colleges, and even at schools outside the Old Dominion.

You can pay into VPEP in a lump sum or in monthly installments until your child reaches college age, or you can participate in the state's five-year pay plan designed for children who have not yet completed the seventh grade. You can change plans and payment options any time you wish, though you will be charged a small fee. Purchasers get refunds with interest if the student dies or becomes disabled, receives a scholarship, or chooses not to attend college.

Federal taxes on the plan's earnings are deferred until tuition is paid, and then the student pays the tax at his or her rate. There is no Virginia state tax on the earnings.

Congress recently passed legislation that expands the definition of expenses that can be prepaid through these plans. Now, not only can you prepay your child's tuition, you can also prepay the expenses for room and board, for tax years that end after August 20, 1996.

For more information about prepaid tuition plans you can contact the College Savings Plans Network, which is the official mouthpiece for these plans. That organization provides updates on what's out there, shares information among existing programs, and keeps track of federal activities and proposed legislation that could affect the plans. You can mail them at P.O. Box 11910, Lexington, KY 40578-1910, or check out their Web site (http://www.collegesavings.org). One advantage to their Web site is that they give you links to each state's prepaid plan.

The Education IRA

In 1997, in a rare act of cooperation, Congress and the president came together to pass a series of tax incentives for your educational needs. One of these programs established the educational Individual Retirement Account. You can set up one of these accounts with a mutual fund company. The rules for how this Education IRA works are quite different from a regular IRA, which has been around for decades and (as you can guess) is used for retirement, not college. For more details on plain old

IRAs, just turn to chapter 5.

With an Education IRA, parents, grandparents, or anyone else can make contributions on behalf of any child who is under the age of 18. The great part of this plan is that it's tax-free as the money grows, and it's still tax-free when it comes time to make withdrawals, as long as you use the cash for qualified university expenses, such as tuition and room and board. If you fail to use the money for education expenses, the earnings will not only be taxed, but you'll have to pay an extra 10 percent penalty, unless the withdrawal is due to death or disability, or if the distribution occurs in a year when your child receives a scholarship.

Unlike a regular IRA, Education IRAs do not allow you to deduct from your taxes the contributions that you put into the account; and each child can receive only $500 per year in contributions. Also, the very well off are limited in how much they can contribute. If you file as a single on your tax return each year, your income has to be less than $95,000 to contribute. If you're married and file jointly, you have to make less than $150,000 annually. Your ability to contribute phases out if you make more than that.

If there's any money left over in your child's Education IRA when he or she turns 30, you'll have to make a choice. That cash must either be rolled over into the Education IRA of another child in the same family, or you'll have to withdraw the money and face all the taxes—and the 10 percent payment penalty.

There's another twist; one that affects what we just talked about with prepaid tuition plans. No contributions to an Education IRA are permitted in years when contributions are made on behalf of the same child to a state prepaid college tuition plan.

As you can see, Education IRAs have advantages for some, but they might not work out as part of your college plan. And even if you decide you want to use this type of IRA, because of the $500 per year contribution limit, the plan at best is only one part in your overall strategy to pay the college bills.

Lifetime Learning Credit and the HOPE Scholarship Credit

The next two changes in the tax law created specials credits, called the Lifetime Learning Credit and the HOPE Scholarship Credit, which are designed for certain types of educational needs. Just as with the Education IRA, these two credits are helpful only as pieces in your overall bill-paying puzzle.

With the Lifetime Learning Credit, you can claim a credit of up to $1,000 each year to pay for college tuition and fees. The actual math says you can claim 20 percent of up to $5,000 in education expenses; that goes up to $10,000 in expenses (meaning a $2,000 credit) starting in the year 2003. The credit applies to expenses paid after June 30, 1998, for schooling that begins after that date. You can even use the credit to pay for graduate or professional school. But the credit can only be used once on each tax return.

The HOPE Scholarship Credit is available only for the first two years of college, and it has a few other variations from the Lifetime Learning Credit. First, the credit will give you up to $1,500 per student for college tuition and fees (100 percent of the first $1,000 in expenses, and 50 percent of the next $1,000 in bills). Second, you must be enrolled in school at least on a half-time basis for a minimum of one academic period during the year. Third, you can use this credit for each child you have in college. You can use this credit for college expenses starting January 1, 1998.

Both credits share some components, including the usual laundry list of restrictions. For both credits you have to meet certain income requirements in order to qualify. These credits are designed for the middle and lower middle class. So you must make less than $40,000 a year if you're single (or $80,000 for joint returns) to get the full credit. After that, the credit gradually phases out and ends for incomes over $50,000 for singles and $100,000 for joint filers. Also, the two credits cannot be taken at the same time for the same student, and what is considered "eligible" college expenses includes tuition and fees, not room and board.

For more information, and to keep track of all these new changes in the tax law, you can click on to the Web site of the IRS (http://www.irs.ustreas.gov). This site will also give you a more thorough rundown of all the other new tax loopholes.

Graduate School or the Inevitable?

Is it worth it? As we discussed at the top of this chapter, you really need to do a cost-benefit analysis. Graduate training is a virtual necessity if you are to become proficient enough with disciplines such as law, health care, chemistry, and the other sciences. But other professions, like writing for television or a newspaper, don't follow that rule. A Ph.D. in a field like journalism is not nearly as valuable a tool in forging ahead at a newspaper as just getting more on-the-job writing experience. But if you plan to go into teaching at the college level (whether it's teaching chemistry, journalism, or whatever) then a Ph.D. makes more sense.

No matter what field you end up studying in, eventually it will come time to pay the bills. If you plan to apply for financial aid, many schools require forms such as the Graduate and Professional School Financial Aid Service (GAPSFAS) form or the Financial Aid Form (FAF). Some schools also require that you fill out their specialized institutional forms.

Universities often offer fellowships, assistantships, grants, work-study, and loans based on academic accomplishment and scholarly promise as well as financial need. Check with the college department that you are applying to, as well as the school's financial aid office. You might also get private sources of aid such as from foundations and corporations. There's government aid as well. Many of the books and Web sites we discussed in earlier parts of this chapter have both graduate and undergraduate financial aid information.

You may get some assistance from your employer if your part-time graduate work serves your company's needs. In the past, when your boss reimbursed you for graduate-level tuition, the benefit was tax-free. Today, it's a little more complicated. If the college classes are required by your employer, or the classes are specifically designed to maintain or advance your current job, then you'll pay no taxes on the benefit. Otherwise, it's treated as taxable income.

The new tax laws extend how much employer-provided education assistance you can exclude from your income. It's now up to $5,250, although only undergraduate education is covered and the courses must begin before June 1, 2000.

Q & A on Financial Aid Issues

Q. Is financial aid only for the poor?
A. No. Middle-class students get lots of aid.
Even families with incomes of $50,000 to
$100,000 or more can qualify, especially when
several family members are enrolled in college
at the same time. At some schools, the median
income for families who get aid is over $50,000.

Q. How are financial aid awards taxed?
A. Grants that pay for tuition and school supplies are tax-free, as long as
your child is pursuing a degree and not merely taking a few classes. Grant
money that pays for room and board is taxed as the student's income.

Q. Will saving and investing for college hurt the chance for getting
financial aid?
A. Yes, but in the end you'll be far better off if you save and invest.
The formula that's used to estimate your expected family contribution
relies much more on your income than on your savings or investments.
For example, less than 6 percent of a parent's assets are figured in
the EFC calculation. Also, money that's in your retirement fund is not
considered when calculating your federal EFC. The only part that gets
looked at is your current year's retirement contributions, but money
already sitting in a retirement fund is safe. A student's assets do
count more; 35 percent counts toward the EFC. So a family that has
lots of savings will be expected to contribute a little more for college.

Q. Why are college costs rising so much more than inflation?
A. There are several reasons. High on the list is that government sub-
sidies to higher education, in the form of grants and special low-interest
loans, have inadvertently exacerbated the cost problems they meant
to fix. Also, universities have increased their enrollment of students
from less affluent families, which has increased the need for financial
aid. Another reason is that colleges have been forced to spend a lot
for new technology.

The Pluses and Minuses of Going Back to Graduate School to Jump-Start Your Career

Business is another area where a graduate education has its pros and cons. It's a particularly relevant example to use when talking about career jumping and jump-starting. Students getting a master's degree in business (an M.B.A.) used to have only two or three years of work experience before they returned to the ivory tower. Today, the average M.B.A. student has more than 12 years of work experience under his or her belt.

Is it worth it? Attending a full-time M.B.A. program requires an investment of two years (maybe more) and typically more than $100,000 in tuition and forgone earnings. In a recent study, newly minted M.B.A.s saw their salary go up, on average, by less than 20 percent over what they were making before. That compares with a salary jump of 40 percent for M.B.A. grads during the 1980s. The supply and demand for graduates in certain fields like business will always fluctuate. So you need to see what side of the pendulum you're on.

Ronald N. Yeaple has a good book on the subject, called *The MBA Advantage* (Adams Media, 1994). He explores whether it's worth it to pursue an M.B.A. He also ranks the top business schools by financial return on investment. You can go to his Web site (http://www.yeaple.com) for more information and advice.

You can also go to a useful site run by some Harvard Business School students (http://marketspace.hbs.edu/bschoolbuzz) who are peddling books on all aspects of graduate and business education. While the site gives some tips on getting into the best schools, you can basically use it as a recommended reading list for books on deciding whether business school is for you, the joys of networking, and how to extract the most from your education.

Paying Off Those Student Loans

Students are awash in student loan debt, and the amount is increasing exponentially. Families in the United States have incurred more debt to finance college education between 1990 and 1995 than during the 1960s, 1970s, and the 1980s combined. The average student loan debt increased from $8,200 in 1991 to $18,800 in 1997,

and 40 percent of borrowers surveyed said that repaying their student loans has caused them to delay purchasing a home. Only 25 percent of borrowers agreed with that statement in 1991.

As we saw earlier in this chapter, there are several low-interest government loans available, based on need. But there are also private sources of loans, such as from Sallie Mae, Nellie Mae, and PLATO. They offer reasonable rates, though not as good as the need-based government loans.

Another way that families pay the college bills is to tap money out of their home. You can use the equity in your home (usually up to 80 percent of the home's market value, less any remaining mortgage debt) as collateral for a home-equity loan. And if you itemize on your tax form, you can also deduct the amount of loan interest you pay from your taxes. Of course, if you can't repay the loan, you could lose your house.

So how can you manage it all? First on your list should be to figure our how much you can reasonably expect to borrow. If your monthly loan payments are running you more than one-third of what you take in each month, then you should start thinking of ways to cut back. Otherwise, you may find it impossible to eventually dig yourself out of debt. Also, if all your cash is going to pay off others, what will be left to pay for little things like food and shelter?

Luckily, there are some new tax laws in your favor. The interest you pay on student loans is deductible from your taxes for the first 60 months in which interest is payable. The maximum deduction is $1,000 for 1998; that number increases by $500 a year until it reaches $2,500 in 2001. And the deductions are "above the line," meaning you can deduct the interest whether or not you itemize on your tax form. Again, this is one of those breaks that's reserved for the middle class and below. Your income has to be under $40,000 ($60,000 if you file jointly) to get the full benefit.

But whatever you do, don't default on your loans. As we saw in chapter 2, bad debt can ruin your credit report, which in turn can cast a long shadow over your finances for years to come. Also, you can end up paying late fees, increased interest, and court fees if things really get ugly.

YOUR retirement Investments

Of all the investments you have to protect, this is probably the most important because you may not have the earning power to make up any losses when you need this money.

There are many vehicles that are at your disposal to help you as you plan your retirement years. They go by odd-sounding names like 401(k), IRA, Roth IRA, and SEP. And we'll get to all that in this chapter. But it's also important to think about what "retirement" actually means to you. Does it mean not working at all? Does it mean working only part-time on projects you enjoy? Or does it mean something unique only to you? Whatever it means to you, planning ahead is key.

When Should You Start Thinking about Retirement?

No matter what your age, now is a good time to map out what you need to do to prepare for retirement. Of course, there are millions of excuses to wait:

"Why save for retirement now? That's decades away."

"I can barely pay my current bills, much less save and invest for retirement."

"Won't Social Security be my safety net in retirement?"

Put those thoughts out of your mind. This is serious business and you should know what obstacles are out there. First off, you need to know about your retirement needs. Retirement is expensive. If you leave the workforce for good, you'll have to find a way to replace what you made on salary. And don't be fooled into thinking that your expenses will be a lot lower than they are now. Experts estimate that you'll need about 70 to 80 percent of your preretirement income (make that 90 percent for lower earners) to maintain your current standard of living. Otherwise, get ready for lots of government cheese.

Second, don't expect Social Security to bail you out. The Social Security Administration estimates that a single person making $40,000 a year before retirement will get less than 40 percent of that income in today's dollars each year from Social Security after retiring. Remember, you'll need 80 percent of your preretirement income to keep you in the lifestyle you have now. Where will the rest of the money come from? And it gets worse. Social Security will likely pay out less in the decades to come than it does now. That's because as the so-called Baby Boomers reach retirement age there will be too many older people drawing out of Social Security and not enough younger people paying into it.

The math is pretty easy to understand. The Baby Boomers represent 78 million Americans born between 1946 and 1964. That's a huge chunk of the population. And now that most boomers are in their forties and fifties, their golden retirement years are not too far in the future. That means there won't be that many workers to support the Social Security system. In 1950, there were more than 16 people who were working and contributing for every one older person receiving benefits. In 1997, only a little more than 3 people were working and contributing to keep retirees in trim. By the year 2040, when the boomers are all lounging around in retirement condos in Florida, there will be only 2 people working to support them. That scenario is not sustainable, and so the system will eventually be "fixed," whether by reducing benefits, raising taxes, changing eligibility, or a combination of all three.

In any event, you should at least get some idea of how your Social Security payments are growing. If you call the Social Security Administration at (800) 772-1213, you can ask for a free Personal Earnings and Benefits Estimate Statement.

Third, you should remember that the cost of living keeps going up. As we saw in chapter 2, inflation is a silent stalker that follows your money every day—even in retirement. You will need to get your financial act together and start saving and investing because things will be even more expensive in the future. Assuming a 4 percent annual inflation rate, a $20,000 car will cost you almost $65,000 in 30 years. And the $125 you shell out for groceries today will run you more than $400 in three decades.

Fourth, you could live a lot longer in retirement than you might expect. According to government statistics, the average American can expect to live around a quarter century more after he or she leaves work and gets the gold watch.

How are you going to pay the bills for a quarter century if you don't have a salary coming in? The answer is you're not. The only way you can ever expect to retire eventually is to set up a strategy that relies on several different "salaries" coming in. On top of Social Security benefits, you need to find out about what kind of pension or profit-sharing plan your employer has. Next you need to see if your employer offers a tax-sheltered savings plan such as a 401(k). You also need to investigate retirement investment vehicles that have special tax treatment, like IRAs. We'll explore each one of these in detail as this chapter goes forward.

Investment Strategies to Help Pay for Retirement

Just like investing for your college needs, successfully investing for retirement is not that hard if you start early. If you're just out of school and in your early twenties, you may have mere pennies to invest, but you have 40 years to work. Great. As we saw in chapter 3, you can get into many strong performing mutual funds with just a small monthly cut from your paycheck. And with four decades to invest, you can afford to take some risk in your investment strategy. That means you can investigate which aggressive growth and long-term growth mutual funds might fit your taste and tolerance. You could also look into spreading a little money internationally, since many regions and countries have such high long-term growth potential. You can also dabble in buying individual stocks, though beginning investors should stick with a full-service broker for a little hand-holding and advice.

If you're in your late twenties or early thirties, you may have a little more money in the bank, but the clock is starting to tick. Stocks and stock mutual funds are still the way to go, and you need to be more consistent in contributing to your nest egg. You can also look at index mutual funds and growth and income funds, depending on how much risk you're comfortable with.

And if you're in your forties or fifties, it's go time. You're at risk of falling into the same trap as the rest of the Baby Boomers who saved too little, spent too much, and now realize that they don't have enough cash to retire. Right now many of them are taking too much risk in their investments to make up for lost time. You shouldn't concentrate all your investment dollars in stocks and stock mutual funds at this point. Rather, you need to balance your risks by allocating part of your portfolio to bonds, bond mutual funds, and money market funds. Otherwise, a stock market drop could really devastate your nest egg. As you get older, a steady stream of income from your investments should be your best friend.

How should you allocate your investment dollars between retirement and nonretirement investment vehicles? As you'll see later in this chapter, there are many special tax incentives built into these retirement investments. But there are restrictions, such as penalties for early withdrawal, and other problems that you need to be aware of.

And you need to be careful of how much money you tie up, because you probably also have other long-term needs, such as a home and your kid's college education.

With some retirement investments you really can have too much of a good thing. For example, if your 401(k) grows to $1.6 million by the age of 50, or $1.4 million by the age of 60, you don't want to put any more cash in. Otherwise, you could be subject to a 15 percent excise tax once it's reinstated in the year 2000. On top of that tax, you'll also have to deal with federal and state income taxes.

Most of you probably won't accumulate that much of a nest egg, but it's a lot easier to get there than you might think. Someone making just $25,000 a year, who dutifully stuffs 10 percent of her salary into her 401(k) starting at the age of 25 (and gets a 10 percent rate of return), will get hit with the penalty by age 64.

Employer Pensions

When you're talking about pensions, they basically fall into two distinct categories: defined-benefit plans and defined-contribution plans. In defined-contribution plans, such as 401(k)s and employee stock ownership plans, the value of your pension fluctuates according to the value of the investment. Generally, you or your employer or both contribute to your plan, sometimes at a set rate, like 5 percent of your earnings annually. We'll dissect these plans next.

But first, let's make a quick run through defined-benefit plans and the rights you have to this money. With these plans, the benefit you get at retirement is clearly defined and will not fluctuate with the undulations of the stock market. The amount you get is sometimes a set dollar amount, like $100 per month at retirement. Usually, though, it's calculated based on your salary and years of service, such as 1 percent of your average salary over the last five years of employment for every year of service at the firm.

The federal government sets certain minimum standards for pension plans. Under the Employee Retirement Income Security Act of 1974 (also called ERISA), employers who offer pension plans must provide participants in the pension with information on the plan's features and funding. Also, ERISA dictates that pensions must

meet standards for participation, vesting, benefit accrual, and funding. In the worst case scenario, ERISA also gives you the ability to sue for benefits.

With defined-benefit plans, ERISA has an added role. It created the Pension Benefit Guaranty Corporation (PBGC for short), which is charged with insuring most defined-benefit pensions. Plans not covered include those of professional service firms, such as doctors and lawyers, who have a handful of employees. Otherwise, if your employer is having financial trouble, PBGC will come to your rescue.

If your employer no longer has the cash to support the pension plan, or there are other problems, the PBGC will step in and take over the plan. It reviews the plan's records to determine what benefits each person will get. Once the PBGC completes its review, it will notify you in writing as to how much of a pension you can expect, as well as the rights you have to appeal its decision. Your pension benefit will depend on several factors, including your age, the provisions of your plan, and how your employer funded the plan before it was taken over.

It's important to note that the PBGC guarantees only a "basic benefit", it does not cover health care, vacation pay, or severance pay. Your benefit amount will be unique to you, but the maximum guaranteed amount, for example, in 1998 was $2,880 per month for a worker who retired at age 65.

For more information on what the PBGC can do for you, you can write the organization at: PBGC, Technical Assistance Division, 1200 K Street, NW, Suite 930, Washington, DC 20005-4026, or call (202) 326-4000. If you have specific questions about your plan or your benefits, though, you should first contact your pension plan's administrator or your employer.

Employee Stock Ownership Plans

Many employers offer employee stock ownership plans (ESOPs) to give their employees a stake in the growth of the company. In fact, Congress created ESOPs to encourage employee participation in corporate ownership. At retirement, or when you leave the firm, you might end up with a nice little chunk of change if your company's stock is successful. Of course, if your company takes a fall, your benefit could be slim to none.

Here's how ESOPs work: You may get company stock through a payroll deduction each month, or the firm may give you shares based on how much it pays you, say 5 to 10 percent of your salary. As the value of your company's stock grows over time, you don't have to worry about paying taxes. They don't come due until you take the money out.

Just as with other employer benefits, you have certain rights. Under the law, your employer has to explain the details of how the plan works, plus what your rights and obligations are. So check out what your employer offers, not just with these stock ownership plans but with the company's regular pension plans. You may find some great opportunities to build your nest egg. But always be wary of the risks, and ask what the worst-case scenario could be.

401(k) Plans

This type of retirement plan is pretty simple to understand, and it can be quite profitable. Don't be put off by the odd-sounding name; 401(k)s have this moniker simply because they are named after a section of the Internal Revenue Code that was added in 1978. They also have an equally funny-sounding cousin, called 403(b) plans. The 403(b) plan was designed for employees at nonprofit, charitable, religious, and educational organizations. Both the 401(k) and the 403(b) plans have been wildly popular since they were created. In the early 1980s, there were less than 2,000 plans in existence. Today there are well over 100,000 plans.

A 401(k) plan is an account set up by your employer that is earmarked for your retirement. You have the choice of contributing to this account, either in fixed dollar amounts or as a percentage of your salary, up to a maximum amount that is adjusted up each year to account for inflation. In 1998, the maximum was $10,000 a year. Your employer also has the option of matching your contributions. Worker-friendly companies tend to mach your contributions dollar for dollar, which is quite generous. Other firms may match only 25 cents to 50 cents for every dollar you contribute.

The money you and your employer put into your 401(k) account can be invested in several ways: stocks and stock mutual funds, bonds and bond mutual funds, or a mix

of all of them. Chapter 3 details the risks and rewards of these investment vehicles and describes the many flavors of stocks and bonds that you can invest in. The 401(k) account gives you another option; you can put your money in a guaranteed investment contract. These contracts (nicknamed GICs) let you know beforehand what your investment return will be. Of course, that lowers the risk in the account, but it also reduces the rewards that are possible with a more aggressive approach.

The advantages to 401(k)s include the fact that you get to set aside pretax income to invest and that the money inside the account gets to grow free from taxes until you retire (when you'll probably be in a lower tax bracket) or take the money out. But don't take the money and run too soon. There is generally a penalty for early withdrawal, that is, withdrawals if you leave your firm before age 55. There are exceptions, though. Your plan may permit you to take money out on account of severe disability. Also, your plan may let you borrow from your 401(k) account.

These plans have basically allowed employers to shift much of the financial and administrative responsibility for retirement benefits to their employees, which is both good and bad. The good part is that if you choose your investments wisely and have the discipline to make consistent contributions, your retirement nest eggs can grow much faster than under a traditional employer pension. The bad part is that now the monkey is on your back to make the most of your retirement money. You have to be your own retirement expert. Unfortunately, many employees are not taking full advantage of 401(k)s. Several academic and business studies show that while many companies offer these plans, only a small percentage of employees actually participate or, when they do participate, make significant contributions.

IRAs: An Introduction

Individual Retirement Accounts are do-it-yourself retirement plans, and they now come in a variety of flavors to suit the needs of different kinds of investment and retirement needs. You have regular IRAs, which have been around since 1974, Roth IRAs, which are the new kid on the block (and we'll look at them next), and Education IRAs, which we checked out in chapter 4. They all have their unique advantages and disadvantages.

First, let's take a look at the plain vanilla variety. Regular IRAs allow you to contribute up to $2,000 a year to your account, and the money grows tax-free. You can make contributions in a lump sum or in installments. You can also decide each year whether or not you want to contribute. But keep in mind that you can't make up missed contributions in later years. You can set up an IRA with a bank, credit union, broker, or mutual fund company.

You may also be able to deduct your annual $2,000 contribution from your taxes if you meet certain requirements. One way to reap this benefit is if you're not covered under an employer pension. But even if you have an employer-sponsored retirement plan, such as a 401(k), you may still make deductible contributions as long as your adjusted gross income is $30,000 or less (for singles) or $50,000 or less (for couples). Deductibility phases out once you get to $40,000 and $60,000, respectively.

The maximum income limits for deducting your contribution changes each year to reflect the cost of living. So for 1999, the maximum for full deduction is $31,000 for singles and $51,000 for joint filers. But by 2002, for example, the maximum will rise to $34,000 and $54,000, respectively.

Even if you're not able to deduct the contribution from your taxes, IRAs still make a lot of sense. All the money you stash in your IRA, plus all the earnings that get reinvested, can grow without being reduced each year by taxes. This creates a wonderful effect on your money, known as tax-deferred compounding. Consider the effects of tax-deferred compounding if you make a $2,000 contribution each year from age 35 to age 65. After 30 years, and assuming an 8 percent annual return, your tax-deferred investment would be worth over $226,500. If that same investment had been subject to taxes each year, you would have lost $75,000 on the deal.

Of course, when you eventually withdraw the money you'll get hit with taxes, but you'll still come out ahead. Even if you took all the cash out at once and paid taxes at 28 percent, your nest egg would still be over $163,000, which is $10,000 more than if the money had been in a taxable account. So is it worth $10,000 to be a consistent and smart investor? You betcha.

Except for higher education expenses and certain first-time home buying expenses, you'll get hit with a 10 percent penalty for any withdrawals you make before you are

59-1/2 years old. It's also important to remember that you can't keep your money tied up in IRAs forever. Under the law, you must stop making contributions and begin taking distribution from your IRA when you're 70-1/2 years old.

One new twist in the tax law helps married couples. A spouse who is not covered by an employer-sponsored retirement plan can now make deductible IRA contributions even if the other spouse is covered. Of course, as with most other government loopholes, there is an income test. The benefit phases out between $150,000 and $160,000 of joint adjusted gross income.

And there's another point to remember. You are not forced to keep your cash in the same IRA account for decades and decades. If your chosen investment, say an IRA invested in a mutual fund, is not making the kind of money you thought it would, you have the right to transfer that money from one mutual fund to another. As long as you never touch the cash during the transfer, you can do this as many times as you wish

Roth IRAs

Roth IRAs were created in 1997 and are named after Senator William Roth of Delaware. Starting in 1998, you can contribute up to $2,000 to a Roth IRA, or 100 percent of your earned income (if your earned income is less than $2,000). The Roth also has an income test to determine how much you can contribute. You can put in the full $2,000 if you have at least $2,000 earned income and your adjusted gross income is $95,000 or less (for singles) or $150,000 or less (for joint filers).

Eligibility phases out once your adjusted gross income reaches $110,000 for singles and $160,000 for couples. Also, you can't put $2,000 each into a Roth IRA and a regular IRA; you can put in only $2,000 total. If you file a joint tax return, your spouse also may contribute up to $2,000 to a separate account, as long as your joint income is $4,000 or more, even if one spouse has no earned income.

The money you contribute is always nondeductible, but your earnings grow tax-free. Once you've owned a Roth IRA for five years, you may withdraw the money after you're 59-1/2 years old or to pay qualifying first-time home-buying expenses. And the beauty is, your tax rate on these withdrawals is zero.

This tax-free status has its limits. If you are 59-1/2 years old or older and have had the Roth IRA for less than five years, your withdrawals are taxed at your income tax rate (though you won't have to worry about any 10 percent payment penalty). If you're under 59-1/2 years old and have had the Roth IRA for less than five years, you get clobbered with the 10 percent penalty, plus withdrawals are taxed as ordinary income.

Unlike with regular IRAs, the Roth IRA does not require that you take distributions after reaching 70-1/2 years of age. And if you have earned income, you can even keep on making contributions to the Roth IRA.

Roth IRAs versus Regular IRAs

In this prize-fight everybody wins. You just need to know which type of IRA best serves your needs. And that really depends on your personal financial situation: how much you make, how much you're taxed (and how much you'll be taxed in the future), and whether your employer provides a retirement plan at work.

For example, if you can deduct your contributions and expect to be paying far less in taxes at retirement age than you do now, then a regular IRA could be better for you than a Roth IRA. That's because of the tax advantages of deducting your contributions and how that can outweigh the taxes you'll pay upon withdrawal.

But if you're in the group of people who can't deduct your contributions, and you don't expect your taxes to go down substantially, then a Roth might be the right choice, especially if you make consistent $2,000 annual contributions. The reasoning here is that with the Roth IRA all the money you withdraw is tax-free (as long as you follow the rules we just discussed). But with regular IRAs, you have to face the full fury of the IRS when you make withdrawals, even if you follow the rules and jump through the hoops. All other factors being equal, a Roth IRA will always give you a better deal than a regular, and nondeductible, IRA.

Rolling Retirement Money into an IRA

As we've seen, there are a wide variety of retirement plans offered by employers. But in today's economy people are constantly bouncing from job to job. So what do you do about your employer-sponsored retirement money when you change jobs?

If you let your firm simply make the check payable to you, then you'll automatically trigger a 20 percent tax withholding penalty on the entire amount that is distributed to you. Although you can get that back when you fill out your tax return, you'll also be subject to a 10 percent penalty if you get early distributions because you retire early or switch jobs.

Fortunately, this tax trap is easy to thwart. Just have your employer send the funds directly to an IRA that you've picked out, or have the check sent to you but be sure that it's made payable to the IRA account. This strategy will work for your 401(k) plan, employee stock ownership plan, or other qualified retirement plan, and you have 60 days to do it. And when you roll the plan into an IRA you don't have to worry about a 20 percent withholding or a 10 percent early withdrawal penalty.

The other option is to have your old employer roll the money into your next employer's retirement plan, although you need to check with your new boss to make sure the company permits this. Even if it does, they don't *have* to do this for you.

If you already have a regular IRA and decide that the Roth IRA is the better route to go, you have the choice of converting your regular IRA assets into a Roth. You can convert whatever percentage of your regular IRA that you wish: there is not a set requirement. But remember that you need to meet an income test (you have to have an adjusted gross income of $100,000 or less) in order to qualify for converting your IRA. And married couples filing separately are not allowed to make the conversion.

If you have money in an employer-sponsored retirement plan, such as a 401(k), there is also a sneaky way to convert that money into a Roth IRA. While you can't make a direct conversion, you can roll the 401(k) money into a regular IRA and then convert the regular IRA into a Roth.

Once you make the switch, tax is due on any accumulated earnings (which, if you've had the money invested for many years, could be a substantial tax bite) and deductible contributions, but not on nondeductible contributions. Also, once you've switched to the Roth IRA, your money has to stay there for at least five years to avoid penalties.

If you have to liquidate existing retirement assets to pay off the tax bill, then you may want to shy away from making the Roth conversion. That's because you'll lose a chunk of your retirement money that could have grown tax-free, and if you're younger than 59-1/2 years old, you could be subject to a 10 percent premature withdrawal penalty on the amount you use to pay the tax. So for the Roth conversion to make sense, you have to be sure you can pay the taxes using money from your savings.

No matter which flavor of IRA you pick, be sure to keep the following information in mind. When you sign on to an IRA, you'll have to choose someone to be your beneficiary. That's the person who will receive the value of your IRA if you should die. You can pick more than one person (you can even choose a charity to get the cash), but be sure to pick a beneficiary, because if you don't have one, then the value of your IRA can be subject to estate taxes.

Also, be smart about what kinds of investments you put into an IRA. You don't want to load up your IRA with investments such as municipal bonds and variable annu-

ities. Even outside of an IRA these vehicles are shielded from income taxes. So there's no benefit to putting them into one. Rather, you should fill your IRA with investments such as stocks and stock mutual funds, which would otherwise cost you in taxes.

Keoghs

If you're self-employed, or if you're moonlighting, you can put money into a Keogh plan. This is true even if you already contribute to an IRA and are covered under an employer-sponsored pension. Keoghs get their name from the congressman who created them in 1962.

Just as with an IRA, you go to a bank, broker, or mutual fund company to fill out the paperwork. You can then fill your Keogh with many types of investments, including stocks, bonds, or mutual funds. With Keoghs you can deduct your contributions, and the earnings from the account grow tax-free until you retire.

Keoghs come in two basic types: defined-contribution and defined-benefit. With a defined-contribution Keogh you can contribute up to around 13 percent of your income. Defined-benefit Keoghs allow you to fund up to 100 percent of your annual income, although there are certain limitations.

Penalties for early withdrawals from Keoghs are similar to the hit you'll take with other retirement plans. With a few exceptions, pulling your money out before you're 59-1/2 years old and have retired will cost you a 10 percent penalty.

SEPs

Simplified employee pension plans (also called SEPs) are similar to Keogh plans, though they're simpler to set up and administer. With a SEP you can set aside self-employment income in a tax-sheltered account. You can contribute up to around 13 percent of your income, and there are no income limits for deducting your contributions from your taxes.

Just as with a 401(k) or an IRA, you have the option to vary how much you con-

Use the Roth for College

When it comes to college financing, the Roth IRA has some clear advantages. You can use the Roth as an effective college-saving vehicle because you can use this money to pay for university tuition and pay nothing in taxes. That assumes, though, that you've had a Roth IRA for at least five years and that you're older than 59-1/2 years of age. Otherwise your earnings will be taxed.

Of course, you have to compare these Roth benefits to what is offered with other types of IRAs. New tax law changes have made the regular IRA more competitive. As of 1998 you can make early withdrawals for education without paying a 10 percent penalty, although earnings will still be taxed.

There is also the new Education IRA, which lets you make withdrawals anytime tax-free and penalty-free provided the proceeds are used for higher education. The big downside here is that you can chip in only $500 per child every year. So research the options that are out there and find out what's best for your unique financial situation.

tribute each year, or you can miss a year if you want. And you have the same investment choices and transfer capabilities as with an IRA. SEPs generally cannot be tapped before you're 59-1/2 years old without triggering a 10 percent penalty. And you have to start drawing from your SEP funds when you reach 70-1/2 years of age.

There also used to be a variation of the SEP called a SARSEP. These plans were abolished a few years back, however, when Congress decided to create the "Savings Incentive Match Plan for Employees," also called a SIMPLE plan. With a SIMPLE-IRA, for example, employees at a business with 100 or fewer people in the firm can reduce their taxable income by the amount they contribute.

Where to Go for Retirement Information

For background information on retirement and retirement planning, all you have to do is pick up the phone, walk to your nearest library, or click on your mouse.

There are several good government sources to tap into. The U.S. Labor Department's Pension and Welfare Benefits Administration is the body that administers and regulates private pensions. Their address is: 200 Constitution Ave., NW, Washington, DC 20210. They also have a publication hotline with lots of informative brochures: (800) 998-7542. You can reach them online as well (http://www.dol.gov/dol/pwba/).

You can contact the Social Security Administration at (800) 772-1213, or go to their Web site (http://www.ssa.gov). They have many pamphlets that can explain all the details of what you can expect from Social Security, including what earnings limits you may face if you're still working while you collect your benefits.

The Employee Benefit Research Institute (EBRI) is a great place for background data (http://ebri.org). Search this website and you can find many informative fact sheets that will give you a bird's-eye view of such topics as women and retirement, and recent changes to IRAs.

American Association of Retired Persons (AARP) has over 30 million members. Their address is 601 E Street, NW, Washington, DC 20049.

The Metropolitan Life Insurance Company (MetLife) has an interesting Internet site called "Life Advice" (http://www.lifeadvice.com). You can get an education here on financing and enjoying retirement.

Annuities

Annuities come in all different shapes and sizes. They are basically financial contracts with insurance companies that you can use as a source of retirement income. Deffered annuities, for example, are a good choice if you have many years before you retire. With this plan, you can postpone shelling out income taxes on your annuity earnings until you withdraw the money at retirement. And you can contribute as little or as much as you want each year.

When you retire, you can enjoy your deferred annuity money in several ways. You can get paid in a lump sum, you can take it as you need it, or you can receive a regular stream of income. If you choose the steady periodic payment option, you can spread your distributions out over the length of your lifetime, no matter how long that is. And the tax liability can also be spread out over your lifetime.

As with all retirement options, there are penalties if you go against the rules that govern annuities. If you withdraw your deferred annuity cash before you are 59-1/2 years old, the IRS will usually stick you with a 10 percent payment penalty. In addition, the insurance company who handles your annuity can slap you with its own special fees.

Just What Is "Retirement"?

The word "retirement" is so ingrained into our language that it's hard to imagine a time when retirement was not a fact of life. But the concept of full-time retirement is really quite new. Up until about 100 years ago there were no retirement plans, no pension plans, no nothing. Older Americans simply worked until a ripe old age and then withdrew gradually from the labor force. They were then supported by their children and other family members.

The first pension plan in the United States was created by American Express in 1875. By the early part of this century employer pension plans began to gain in popularity, and the growth in these plans was spurred on by federal laws that gave employers powerful tax incentives to set up pensions. By 1940, about 15 percent of private-sector workers were covered by a pension. The idea of employee retirement benefits

Retirement Worksheet: How Much Will You Need?

How much you need depends on many factors, and each person has different sources of income. But a good way to get a bird's-eye view of what kind of money you have and what kind of money you'll need is to make a list:

What will your assets be worth?

1. Social Security benefits estimate = _____

2. Pension benefit estimate = _____

3. Retirement investments = _____

4. Home value = _____

5. Other assets = _____

These are in today's dollars. You'll need to project what you think inflation will be like in the 10, 20, or 30 years when you retire (say, 3 to 4 percent annually), and estimate a reasonable rate of return for your investments (say 8 to 10 percent annually).

What will your costs be?

Take 80 to 90 percent of your current income _____ and then project how that number will grow with inflation over your desired number of years.

These simple calculations will give you just a taste of what you have going for you. There are a number of good Web sites that you can use to calculate to the dollar how much you'll need to save to meet your retirement goals.

Many companies, such as Fleet Bank (http://www.fleet.com), Charles Schwab (http://www.schwab.com), Vanguard (http://www.vanguard.com), and Merrill Lynch (http://www.merrill-lynch.ml.com/personal/retire/ retworksheet.html), let you do the math on your retirement needs. The site run by Money Advisor (http://www.moneyadvisor.com) also has useful calculators. Remember, though, that there is always a subtle sales pitch intertwined with these free worksheets.

became more and more the rule rather than the exception after World War II and into the boom years of the 1950s. More than one-third of workers were covered by then.

Through the 1970s Congress created even more retirement incentives, such as the IRA and 401(k), and it set up standards and safeguards for existing employer pension plans to guarantee that workers could enjoy a long and happy retirement. It's no wonder, then, that by 1980 almost half of all private-sector workers were covered by a pension.

But then a series of laws in the 1980s began to chip away at the incentives of some retirement plans. In 1986, for instance, Congress made substantial changes to the rules that govern IRAs and 401(k)s by restricting 401(k) salary reduction contributions and restricting who can deduct their IRA contribution from their taxes. By 1990 the number of private-sector workers covered by a pension dipped back to 43 percent.

This little history lesson is just to suggest that you need to keep an open mind about what constitutes "retirement." The rules are always changing and new trends are always emerging. For example, for the past generation there has been a steady decline in the number of defined-benefit pensions (the ones where your employer does all the worrying and investment planning) and a rise in defined-contribution plans (where you

pick the investments), like the 401(k). This makes employees far more responsible for building their own nest egg and ensuring their own retirement. Also, the labor market in this country is shifting, and many of the industries that offered the broadest pension coverage in the past are now in decline.

The low savings rate among Americans is another strike against being able to retire with any kind of financial security. Over the past 30 years, personal savings has consistently fallen and now stands at less than 5 percent; that's only about one-third of what you need to do if you want to retire and still enjoy a comparable standard of living.

The Three-Legged Stool of Retirement Planning

When it comes to planning for retirement, financial advisers always talk about the "three-legged stool" that represents how to build your nest egg. The three legs are your pension, your savings and investments, and your Social Security benefits. As we've just seen in this chapter, each leg is vital for retirement, but each leg has its own inherent instability. The exact size of your employer pension is less guaranteed than in years past, your savings and investment plans work well only if you start early, and Social Security benefits are no safety net, may be significantly smaller in the future, and can be subject to earnings limits.

Further complicating your retirement plans is trying to figure out how long your retirement money is going to have to last. The good news is that people, on average, live a lot longer today than at any other point in history. In America, a 65-year-old today has about a 1 in 4 chance of living until the age of 90. In 1940, the odds were just 1 in 14. And with the invention of new medicines and therapies, many young people today have good odds of living well past 100.

So if you completely retire at age 65 and run off to go fly fishing, you'll have decades and decades of life and living to pay for with no salary coming in. You'll have to rely on your three-legged stool for financial security. Will it be enough? Maybe. Maybe not.

Consider "Part-Time" Retirement

In many ways it makes sense to forget about the conventional idea of retirement and think about part-time retirement mixed in with some type of work. There are two good reasons for this. First, a part-time job can provide a helpful piece of side income to ensure that you have the funds to pay the bills and live the life you want to live. And there are so many choices open for you. You can do a part-time gig based on your former profession, perhaps by consulting or teaching. Or you can change professions completely. And second, you'll get very bored, very quickly once you stop working. Most people need to work to feel a sense of accomplishment and meaning in their lives.

Some people go in the opposite direction and actually retire early from their job. The problem there is that the current retirement system discourages early retirement. All three legs of the retirement stool include penalties for early withdrawal. For example, while most employer pension plans will let you collect your pension as early as age 55, you'll probably get a third less in benefits. With a retirement investment, like an IRA, there is generally a 10 percent penalty for withdrawals before you are 59-1/2 years old. And if you tap into Social Security as early as age 62, you'll receive only 80 percent of what you would have gotten if you had waited until the "normal" age of 65. What's more, the "normal" retirement age is not uniform, and it's higher for some people.

So if you want to leave your current job, that's fine. You shouldn't be stuck doing something that you don't love. Just be sure to have another type of job lined up and don't tap your retirement funds early unless you're prepared to face the consequences.

HEALTH *insurance* and *disability* INSURANCE

CHAPTER SIX

You need to protect your income from the threat of sickness or disability, and the way to do this is with health insurance and disability insurance. You may be young and strong, but illness or injury can strike at any time.

You need strategies to be sure your earning power is preserved if something happens to prevent you from working.

Health Issues You'll Have to Deal With

During your lifetime you'll use the services of a doctor more times than you care to think about. When you're young, usually the only contact you have with a physician is for regular physicals and immunization shots. The doctor pokes and prods a little and that's that. Moreover, since your parents probably paid the bills, you most likely never gave health insurance a second thought.

But as you get older you find yourself making more and more pit stops at the doctor's to check an ache here or a pain there. After a while the bills start piling up. That's why it's so important to choose the right health insurance plan for your needs.

There are many different health issues that you'll have to deal with, and while some procedures will be covered by insurance, others will have to be paid for out of your pocket. What's covered and what's not covered will depend on what type of health insurance plan you have, where you have it, and whose plan you're under.

Depending on your plan, the list of covered services might include physical therapy, respiratory therapy, radiology, mental health care, and, of course, surgical care and anesthesia. Many plans also provide for some preventive services, such as routine check-ups, immunizations, and screenings for potential health problems. The list of services not covered might include birth control devices, treatment for obesity, and cosmetic surgery, unless the procedure is used to correct a birth defect.

Then there are other services that don't fit neatly into either category. Orthodontic care is a good example. These services include the braces and brackets that make kids frown and the retainers that adults wear to keep their teeth in just the right position. Insurance for orthodontic services is not available on an individual basis, but many people get coverage through their employer.

According to the American Association of Orthodontists (AAO), only a small percentage of small businesses offer their employees dental coverage, much less orthodontic benefits. The numbers break down to only one in five small companies covering dental care, and only 40 percent of those plans give orthodontic benefits. Large firms tend to be more generous, with around 70 percent offering dental coverage, and 75 percent of those providing an orthodontic benefit.

This coverage is not just important to your kids. Many adults (about 25 percent, according to the AAO) get braces, too, for corrective or cosmetic reasons. And considering the costs involved, it's important to ask questions and find out what your insurance covers and excludes from coverage. Orthodontic care can range from $2,000 to $5,000, depending on what's involved and where you live.

Health Insurance: An Introduction

The health insurance industry as we know it today is really quite different from what it was only a generation ago. And if you go back a little further, you'll find a time before Blue Cross and Blue Shield. In 1847, the Massachusetts Health Insurance Company of Boston became the first insurer to offer "sickness" insurance. By the 1870s, railroads and other industries were furnishing company doctors to their workers to keep them healthy. The doctors' pay came from deductions from the workers' wages.

In 1929, a group of schoolteachers worked out a deal with Baylor Hospital in Dallas, Texas, where they would be given a hospital room and certain medical services for a predetermined monthly cost. This plan is considered the forerunner of Blue Cross plans. And in 1973, Congress established the structure of what are now known as Health Maintenance Organizations, or HMOs.

Traditional versus Managed Care

Just 25 years ago, most people in America were covered by health insurance plans know as "indemnity" insurance. These traditional indemnity plans, which are also called "fee-for-service" plans, give you the choice of getting your medical care from any doctor and any hospital you wish. No questions asked. And when the bill arrives, both you and your insurer split the costs.

Today, however, more than 80 percent of those with private health insurance are covered by one of the many types of "managed care" plans. They go by acronyms like HMO, PPO, and POS. These plans are designed to contain medical costs by restricting which doctors and hospitals you can rely on for care.

There is no "best" health insurance plan. When comparing health plans, you should ask lots of questions to find out who offers what. First off, find out what services are covered, and what services are not (they're usually called "exclusions"). For example, most plans, whether they are fee-for-service or managed care, won't pay for experimental treatments. And each insurer has its own definition of what's considered experimental.

Also, ask for a list of what doctors and hospitals are included under the health plan. If you've been seeing the same physician for 20 years and she is not on the list, then that's a serious consideration. You should also find out if the plan imposes limits on how you'll have to pay for treatment of a major illness, and if the insurer places a cap on how much it will pay out in benefits over your lifetime.

Currently almost 225 million Americans have some sort of health insurance, whether it be indemnity or managed care. That compares with almost 42 million souls without a health plan. People's attitudes about health insurance are always changing, and sometimes they have no basis in reality. For example, according to a recent survey by the Employee Benefit Research Institute and Mathew Greenwald & Associates, more than 80 percent of those polled said that health care costs had gotten worse over the last five years. But the fact is that over the past five years health care costs generally have remained the same and in some areas have actually decreased. That's why it's so important to get the facts on health care and make an educated decision in picking a health plan.

How Much Health Insurance Do You Need?

The answer really depends on how old you are, where you are in life, and how healthy you are. The health insurance needs of someone who is married with three kids is different from the needs of a retiree or a single twentysomething just starting out.

In general, though, you'll want a health plan with a high maximum lifetime benefit. That way a catastrophic illness won't wipe you out financially. If the benefits cap is too low, you might eventually run up more in medical bills than your insurer will pay. At that point, you're on your own. Also, the "stop-loss" limit (which is the cap on your out-of-pocket medical costs for any given year) on your plan should be a number you are comfortable with. You need to realize, though, that the lower the stop-loss limit the higher your monthly premium will be.

How large your deductible will be and how much coinsurance you'll have to deal with are two other considerations. The "deductible" is just a fancy way of saying how much of your medical bills you initially have to pay each year before your insurer

The Family and Medical Leave Act

In the past few years Congress has passed several pieces of legislation to help people deal with their health care needs. One of these laws, the Family and Medical Leave Act, gives you the right to take off from work to care for a sick family member, or to take care of your own medical needs. In the past, some employees were hesitant to take time away from their office for fear that their boss might fire them for neglecting their work.

Now, under the law, you can leave work for up to 12 weeks without having to worry that your job may be lost in the process. It's important to note that the law applies only to firms with 50 or more employees, though, so if you work for a small company, you may be out of luck.

Also, keep in mind that any leave you take is unpaid leave. And that can really affect your pocketbook. Finally, when you notify your boss that you need to take the time off, be sure to invoke the name of the Family and Medical Leave Act so that your employer clearly knows that you are seeking protection under the law.

steps in to help. As a general rule, the higher the deductible the lower the premium. If you're young, healthy, and single, you may want to look at having a higher deductible so you can reduce your monthly premiums. If you have a family that depends on your health plan, then a lower deductible might make more sense. If you're covered under an employer plan, you may not have a choice.

"Coinsurance" is a term that describes the percentage of the health bills your insurer will pay versus the percentage left for you to pay. The percentage will vary from plan to plan and from medical procedure to medical procedure; a common example is for

services to be covered 80 percent by your insurer and 20 percent by you.

As you get older your questions about how much insurance you require will also have to include the choices involved with getting Medicare. Americans who are 65 years or older (as well as people with certain disabilities) can get hospital and doctor coverage through Medicare, which was set up in 1965. Medicare is divided into two parts, Part A, which covers hospital trips, and Part B, which covers doctor visits.

Whether you realize it or not, you pay for Part A all your life through monthly deductions in your paycheck. So when you hit age 65, you get Part A coverage without paying a premium. Part B will cost you a little, though, and the premium goes up every year. Recently the monthly premium was around $45. You get enrolled in Part B at the time you become eligible for Part A, unless you don't want it. In some areas, people covered by Medicare now have more choices concerning their health plan. They have the choice between indemnity and managed care plans, and they can switch for any reason.

Medicare may not cover all your medical needs, so you may have to purchase additional coverage known as Medigap insurance. By contacting your state's insurance department, you can get a list of what types of plans are out there.

Where Can You Get Health Insurance?

The majority of people get health insurance from their employer or through a family member. Most companies offer a health plan, though what they offer really differs from firm to firm. Some companies ask you to pay part of the monthly premium, other companies give you coverage for free. And some companies give you several types of health plans to choose from, whereas others take a one-size-fits-all approach.

Also, some company plans are self-insured, meaning that they, rather than a health insurance company, assume the risk of health care costs. Currently, around 50 million workers are covered by self-insured plans. It's important to keep that in mind since self-insured employers are exempt from state regulations governing health benefit plans.

If you can't get health insurance through your employer, or if you're self-employed, you still have a few options. Many organizations, such as unions, professional associations, and social or civic groups often offer health plans for members. You should investigate to see if any group you belong to has such a plan. This way you can still be part of a group health plan, which will cost you less than an individual policy.

If an individual plan is the only way to go, then you may want to contact an insurance broker, who can explain what indemnity and managed care plans are available for you. You can also contact your state's division of insurance. Some states provide insurance to small groups and the self-employed. One tax note to remember is that if you're self-employed you can deduct a large part of your health care premium from your taxes. In 1998, the percentage is 45 percent; by 2006 that will rise to 80 percent.

A Look at the Different Types of Health Plans

There are many types of health plans out there, and sometimes it's hard to know what makes each one tick. How are they similar? And how are they different? Some plans have been around for generations. Others are recent arrivals. We will now take a close-up look at indemnity plans, and several managed care plans, including Health Maintenance Organizations (HMOs), Preferred Provider Organizations (PPOs), and Point of Service (POS) plans.

Indemnity Plans

These plans represent the traditional way that health care has been dispensed over the years. You, and not your insurer, get to choose where you get your medical care. You then send your indemnity insurer the bill and they pay part of it. The usual breakdown is they pay 80 percent of the bill and you pay 20 percent.

But it's not that simple. How much they pay (and how much you're left to pay) is based on what they deem to be the "usual and customary" fee for whatever medical

procedure you received. For example, if you get a certain kind of operation that costs you $1,000, your insurer may calculate that the "usual and customary" charge is actually $900. So when they pay 80 percent of the bill what they will actually do is pay 80 percent of $900, not 80 percent of $1,000.

Also, your indemnity insurers won't even start paying your medical bills until you meet a certain deductible, say the first $200 or $300 you rack up in health charges each year.

Indemnity plans generally pay for medical tests and prescriptions, but they may not pay for preventive care, such as checkups. Indemnity plans have been losing popularity for years because they can leave you with high out-of-pockets costs, and because they may not cover all your medical needs. But they do give you the freedom to choose your doctors and your hospitals.

HMOs

These plans were created as a response to what people didn't like about indemnity plans. With HMOs you don't pay a deductible, and you're responsible only for a small fee for most services. For example, office visits may cost only $10 or so. There are low out-of-pocket costs and no claim forms. Plus, HMOs are famous for their attention to preventive care. They provide for regular checkups, cancer screenings, and some plans will even pay you to join a health club.

It's important to note that there is more than one type of HMO. One variety is a "staff-model" HMO. That just means that the plan owns and operates the health care center that they staff with their own paid doctors. The medical center is usually a one-stop shop, where you can see your doctor, get x-rays and lab tests, and even get your prescription filled at their pharmacy. There are also "group-model" HMOs that are similar to the staff-model brand, though the doctors are not employed by the health plan.

Then there are IPAs, "independent practice associations," which are the most popular type of HMO. In this case, the doctors are not under the same roof; they maintain their own practice but agree to accept HMO patients.

When you join an HMO the organization hands you a list of doctors you are allowed to see. You then pick a primary care doctor from that list who becomes the first person you see for your medical needs. If you see a doctor who is not on the plan's list you have to pay the bills yourself. You can see that HMOs impose a number of restrictions on your health choices, but they offer many benefits at the same time.

PPOs

A preferred provider organization is a form of managed care plan, just like an HMO. But PPOs are very different from HMOs and in fact share far more with indemnity plans. When you join a PPO the plan sends you a big book full of doctors in every specialty you can think of. Most likely your current doctor is on the plan's list. If so, that's great. All you have to do is go to your doctor as before and your PPO will pay, say, 80 percent of the bill. You may also have to pay a flat fee, say, $10 for an office visit.

What's more, the doctors and hospitals in the PPO have agreed to accept lower fees for the services they provide. This helps keep down health costs. You can also see a doctor outside the PPO's sphere of influence. The PPO will still pay, but the percentage will be significantly smaller. Also, you may end up having to pay the difference between what the doctor charges and what the PPO deems to be a reasonable fee.

PPOs offer a full range of benefits and have low out-of-pocket costs, but you'll still be stuck filling out paperwork from time to time. In addition, PPOs lack the convenience of having all your medical needs met under one roof. You will also likely pay a deductible of a few hundred dollars each year before the PPO coverage kicks in.

POS

A point of service plan is somewhere in between an HMO and a PPO. As long as you stick with the doctors who are in the POS plan, the procedures for how you pay and what you pay are pretty much like an HMO. There are no deductibles and all you'll have to shell out is a small flat fee for each service.

If you need to see a physician who is outside the plan, the POS looks more like a

PPO. You'll have to deal with deductibles and coinsurance. Just as with an HMO, POS plans ask you to pick a primary care doctor. If your doctor is the one who refers you to a doctor outside the POS, then the plan will still pay most or all of the tab. But if you're the one who decides to go outside the network, that's when the bills will start piling up.

COBRA

Don't worry, this cobra won't bite. COBRA is just an acronym for a bill Congress passed in 1985 called the Consolidated Omnibus Budget Reconciliation Act. Under this law employers with 20 or more employees need to offer continued health coverage to employees who leave the firm and would otherwise be left uninsured. And you can keep this coverage for up to 18 months after you leave your job. If you are married, your spouse and your kids can stay covered up to 36 months.

While COBRA is good news for you because you won't be left stranded without health insurance, there is a catch. What you end up paying in monthly premiums will likely be far more than you were paying while you were on the job. That's because your ex-employer gets to charge you the same rates the company pays for its group plan, plus your ex-employer can tack on a 2 percent administrative fee for its troubles. While you were working, your boss probably subsidized the premiums you paid.

To put COBRA to work for you, be sure to speak up to your employer before you go. You have only 60 days from the end of your employment to exercise your rights under the law. After that, you can't use COBRA. Once you're set up under COBRA, you'll then mail your premium check in each month to maintain coverage.

COBRA isn't only useful if you leave your employer. Recent college graduates who were previously covered by their parents' health plan can also use COBRA as a bridge between when they get their diploma and when they nail their first big job that comes with health benefits. But remember, you can't use COBRA if your coverage was formerly from your college's medical plan.

The Kassebaum-Kennedy Bill

In 1996, two senators (Nancy Kassebaum of Kansas and Edward Kennedy of Massachusetts) on opposite sides of the political spectrum came together to craft legislation that gives you a lot more options when it comes to your health care choices.

In the past if you switched jobs you might have had to worry that you had nowhere to turn if your new company's health plan wouldn't cover you for months and months. Not anymore. Under the Health Insurance Portability and Accountability Act, you can have continuous access to health insurance regardless of any health problems.

The new rules restrict health plans and insurers from denying coverage based on pre-existing conditions, such as medical history, genetic tests, or a disability. To get full protection under the law you must have had health coverage at your old job for at least 12 months and not let your coverage lapse for more than two months (63 days). If you had health coverage for only, say, 6 months, then the law states that your new boss has to count that time against whatever waiting period the new company imposes.

Regardless of other coverage issues, your company can't deny you the same health plan that it offers its other employees and you cannot be dropped for poor health. And if you need to buy individual coverage, insurers who sell individual plans must offer to sell you coverage and they can't charge extra based on your medical history.

While the law gives you more insurance portability as you jump from job to job, keep in mind what's not included. Employers are still not required to offer health insurance to their employees if the company doesn't already have a health plan, and what you end up paying for your coverage can be quite high. According to a General Accounting Office study, people with preexisting conditions who buy individual health insurance often get charged up to 600 percent more than what they'd pay for a group plan premium.

The Kassebaum–Kennedy law also created the trial use of so-called Medical Savings Accounts (or MSAs). These MSAs are meant for self-employed workers, employees at small companies (no more than 50 in the firm), and the uninsured. Think of an MSA as an IRA that you make tax-deductible contributions to and you then use to pay off your medical bills. Any money that you don't have to use in any given year gets to grow with the taxes deferred.

MSAs work with high-deductible indemnity health plans, where the deductible is between $1,500 and $2,250 for singles and between $3,000 and $4,500 for family policies. But keep in mind that the law permits only 750,000 of these MSAs to be set up. And that's on a first-come, first-served basis.

Homework You Should Do Before You Choose a Health Plan

There are lots of different health plans out there, and most are good plans with hard-working doctors. But you always need to be wary of the few bad apples. You need to make sure that you're joining a quality health plan. That means you need to make a few phone calls and ask a few questions.

The first step is to check with federal and state regulatory agencies. For example, indemnity plans are regulated by state insurance commissions. So call up your state's department of health or insurance commission and find out if there have been any problems. Many managed care plans are regulated by federal and state agencies.

The second step is to find out what kind of "accreditation" the health plan has. Accreditation means that the plan meets the specific criteria of an independent organization that reviews quality and standards. Often you'll get a report card that lists the health plan's strong points and weak points. Here is a sample of some of the organizations that accredit health care:

- The National Committee for Quality Assurance accredits HMOs and other managed care organizations. You can reach them at: 2000 L Street, NW, Suite 500, Washington, DC 20036, (800) 839-6487, or click on to their Web page (http://www.ncqu.org).

- The Utilization Review Accreditation Commission checks out PPOs and other managed care networks. They are at: 1130 Connecticut Avenue, NW, Suite 450, Washington, DC 20036, (202) 296-0120.

- The Medical Quality Commission accredits medical groups and IPAs.

They are located at: 310 Old Ranch Pkwy., Suite 205, Seal Beach, CA 90740, (310) 936-1100.

- The Joint Commission on Accreditation of Health Organizations evaluates and accredits over 15,000 health care organizations, including hospitals and ambulatory care services. You can reach them at: One Renaissance Blvd., Oakbrook Terrace, IL 60181, (630) 792-5000.

- The Community Health Accreditation Program accredits home health programs and nursing centers. They are at: 350 Hudson Street, New York, NY 10014, (800) 669-1656, extension 242.

Make Sure Your Doctor Is Properly Licensed

Because you end up putting so much trust in your doctor, it's wise to first check out his or her background. One easy step is to walk over to your local library and open up the book *The Directory of Medical Specialists*. This tome provides biographic information on 400,000 physicians.

Next you can surf to the Web site of the American Medical Association (http://www.ama-assn.org). This site can also give you information about your doctor.

While all doctors have to be licensed to practice medicine, still other doctors go through extra training to get board certified. If you call the American Board of Medical Specialties (800-776-2378) they can get you started on your search for your doctor's board certification.

You may also want to know if your doctor has had to face disciplinary action or has had complaints raised against him. To find out, contact your state's medical licensing board. You can also call your state's Department of Insurance to see if they have received complaints.

Once you have established that you have a doctor you can trust, it's important to make sure that you take charge of the relationship. That means that communications between you two should not be a one-way street. If you don't understand what your

doctor is saying to you, ask her to explain it in another way. And if you have questions for your doctor, always write them down. Otherwise, you may forget one of your questions in the fast-paced environment that is the modern doctor's office.

If you notice symptoms that you feel need your doctor's attention, keep a written log of the problems so you can better explain the situation to your doctor. Also, write down the names of all the medications that you take or have recently taken and note if you had any reaction. Doctors need to know this kind of information so they don't mistakenly prescribe a drug that may cause a bad reaction.

Health Information Online

There's so much juicy information online that it's hard to know where to start. When in doubt go first to a government site called the U.S. Consumer Gateway (http://www.consumer.gov). This site has far more than health information; it also has tips on your home, your money, and product safety. But if you click on to the "health" icon, you'll be transported to a page that offers multiple links and helpful advice.

One link takes you to the Food and Drug Administration's site. There you can get information on health frauds to watch out for and look at data on drug evaluations and research.

Then you should go to "Healthfinder," which is another government site (http://www.healthfinder.gov). Healthfinder provides health news for seniors, infants, minorities and others, and lists links to group-related Web pages. It also answers frequently asked questions on food safety and nutrition and gives advice on how to quit smoking.

The famous Mayo Clinic also has a helpful Web site (http://www.mayohealth.org). It offers information on allergies, Alzheimer's disease, heart disease, and women's health issues. In addition, you can type in the name of whatever medical condition you want information on and the site will spit out several past stories it has written on the subject.

Health Care Power of Attorney

You may not like to think about it, but you may find yourself in a situation where you're no longer able to make important medical decisions for yourself. For example, if you were unconscious and hooked up to life support equipment, what would you want to be done? Would you want to be artificially kept alive indefinitely, or would you rather have the doctors let you die? If you can't speak up for yourself, these decisions will be in the hands of others.

By setting up a health care power of attorney, you are able to designate someone to speak for you. This person can be a family member or close friend, and he or she can interpret your instructions and respond to your changing medical condition. In most states, the person you select, called an agent or proxy, has the power to withdraw life support if that is your choice. So be sure you choose someone who clearly understands and shares your beliefs and wishes.

For a free copy of the paperwork you need to make out a health care power of attorney or a living will, you can call Choice in Dying, an advocate in this field. Their number is (800) 989-9455. You can also contact the bar association in your state or county to see what forms are required in your area to make these medical choices. They also may be able to provide you with copies of the proper forms.

If your health questions deal with your pearly whites, just go to the site of the American Dental Association (http://www.ada.org). You can get consumer information on dental treatments and insurance issues.

And if you want to be a little less conventional about your health care choices, one

good, somewhat alternative site is run by the Integrative Medical Arts Group (http://www.healthwwweb.com). This site has information on acupuncture, as well as links to all sorts of sites concerning herbs and botanical medicine.

Of course, remember that before you take the advice of any online resource, be sure to check it out with your doctor to make sure it's okay.

Disability Insurance: An Introduction

An accident can happen at any time. You could be involved in a car crash that leaves you in a wheelchair. You could be damaged in a mishap at your work site. You could even sustain a permanent injury at the company softball game. And if you were to fall victim to a disability, how would you be able to pay your bills?

That's where disability insurance comes in. This type of insurance comes in many different forms and from several different sources, but basically disability insurance provides income to replace a part of what you were making before the onset of your disability.

If you're single, or if you're self-employed, you should really look into disability insurance. With no one to support you should you fall ill, a disability plan can be part of your safety net. And if you're married, disability insurance is also important. The last thing you want to do is be a drain on your family's financial resources. With a disability plan you'll still have at least some income coming in.

Who Offers Disability Plans and How Much Income Will It Replace?

There are three main sources for disability income: your employer, the federal government, and private insurers. Many employers offer it as part of their fringe benefit package. It may come along with health insurance, a little life insurance, and a transportation stipend. What's more, many employers pay the disability premiums themselves, so you may already have disability insurance and not even know it.

An employer's disability coverage, though, may replace only half the income you were making on the job. Other employer plans are more generous, but even they will not replace all of your income. There's an important point to keep in mind with employers and disability: Before you get to the point where you need to collect disability income, think about your other options. Many employers let you bank sick days if you don't use them all. If your injury is short-term, those sick days may be enough to bridge the gap. Of course, many other firms ask you to periodically draw down on your sick days to avoid this situation. It pays to ask your employer what the policy is beforehand.

The federal government may also provide you with some limited help through Social Security disability insurance. The requirements for getting into this program are strict, and you'll have to go through a lot of paperwork and bureaucracy in the process. But if you successfully jump through all their hoops, Social Security disability insurance can supplement your disability income and replace, say, 50 percent of your previous salary.

There are also a number of private insurers who write disability plans. These plans can fill the gap between what you may get from Social Security and your employer's plan. Private disability plans give you lots of choices as far as how much of the income gap you need filled, and how long you will need the insurance. The cost of your premium will depend on how much income the policy is designed to replace, say, 60 percent or 80 percent, and how long you want the benefits to last, say, one year, or your whole lifetime.

THE AMERICANS WITH DISABILITIES ACT (ADA)

The ADA is another example of Congress and the president coming together to expand your rights. Under the Americans with Disabilities Act, employers with 15 or more employees are required to make reasonable accommodations to individuals with disabilities.

These accommodations include making your workspace more accessible and usable. For example, if you're blind, you can get a computer that responds to voice commands. The ADA is also designed to make it easier for the disabled to get to work. You might have noticed more and more wheelchair ramps being built around large office buildings over the past few years. That's all part of the ADA at work.

How Disabled Is "Disabled," and How Long Must You Wait Before You Collect?

Each of the three different sources of disability insurance—your employer, Social Security, and private insurers—have their own unique definitions of "disabled." You may think that disabled means that you are no longer able to do your current job. But that's a very narrow definition. If you become partially disabled, your company's plan, for example, may merely switch your job requirements to fit whatever work you can still perform, rather than pay out benefits to you.

Social Security, too, finds ways to restrict disability coverage. Under their criteria you have to be unable to do any "substantial" work, not just your present work. If you are able to make more than $500 a month, you may be out of luck. Also, Social Security's disability plan is not meant for the partially disabled. To qualify you must have a disability that will last at least one year. Even then, you can't start collecting at once. You must wait for five months before you are eligible. And the claims process may take up to two years.

Private insurance plans have different layers of disability coverage. You might end up getting "residual" benefits, which means you may be able to do part, but not all, of your current job and still get coverage. Other benefits are based on "presumptive disability," which means that the nature of your disability is sufficiently severe that you qualify for coverage even if you may still be able to stay on the job.

Disability policies give you the option of how long you're prepared to wait before your disability coverage kicks in. As you might expect, the longer you can wait, the lower your premium will be. Given the fact that (knock on wood) you probably won't be involved in the kind of catastrophic accident that would require you to get immediate coverage, you're probably better off opting for a longer time period and keeping your premiums low.

As you go shopping for disability plans, it's also wise to ask each insurer for a sample copy of the coverage it is offering. Buried in the fine print you may find other examples of how ill you have to be, what's included, and what's not.

How to Keep Disability Premiums Low

How much you end up paying on your disability premiums is calculated based on several factors, some of which we've already gone over. But other factors, including what kind of job you have, what kind of risk factors you face, and where you live, also play a role.

One great way to keep your premiums low is to stop smoking. Nonsmokers pay less and with good reason. Also, if you tend to take a lot of sick days at work, you might find yourself with higher premiums.

Other factors that determine your premium may be less easy to control. People who work in a quiet and safe office setting find it a lot easier to get disability coverage than, say, someone who works with dangerous machinery all day.

Also, state regulation of disability plans may cause the insurer to tack on extra costs for coverage. Generally, the more the regulation, the higher the cost is for the insurer to offer the coverage. And so they pass the added costs on to you.

YOUR assets

CHAPTER SEVEN

You have more to protect than cash. Your assets are valuable and are at risk from liability lawsuit, fire, natural disaster, storms, and accidents.

This chapter explains the safeguards you can put in place to avoid the costly expense of replacing your assets. We'll be looking at homeowner's insurance, renter's insurance, car insurance, and more.

Reaching Your Goals and Protecting What You Have

This chapter is about protecting your assets. But the word "asset" is a pretty cold way to describe what we're really going to be talking about. For example, you may think of a home as an asset. But instead, think of it as the fulfillment of one of the major missions of your life. You may have spent a lot of time and a lot of effort and a lot of

financial heartache saving up to buy a home and to purchase all the valuables to go in it. With that in mind, doesn't it make sense to do all you can to protect your assets?

That's where insurance comes into the picture. Yes, it's one more cost you have to tack on to your budget, but once you see that your home is more than an asset, it will be much easier to find the energy it takes to do your homework and choose the right insurance to fit your needs.

Car insurance is another dry topic that nobody likes to talk about. But here again, your car is more than an asset, not to mention the lives and well-being of all the souls who will be riding in that vehicle. Once you put things into the proper perspective, it's easy to see why you need to understand insurance issues.

So far in this book we've talked about saving and investing techniques to reach your financial goals. Now we're going to explore ways to protect and maintain what you have. And one basic way to start the protection process is to find a secure place to store your basic personal documents. These documents include a complete inventory of what items you have in your home, the title to your car, and papers like your birth and marriage certificates, and your will.

A complete inventory of your home should include the serial number, size, and make of each item, plus a picture of the item if it is valuable enough. You should also write down how much you paid (a receipt is even better) and where and when you purchased it. Every time you add to your collection of valuables, you should fill out this paperwork.

A safe deposit box is the place to store these documents. Remember, a fire or a burglary could wipe out all of your records. The safe choice is to find a separate place to protect your personal information.

Homeowner's Insurance: An Introduction

When you buy homeowner's insurance you're doing more than just getting a one-size-fits-all policy. There are several terms you first have to understand so that the insurance process makes some sense.

For example, you'll have the choice of insuring your home for either the replacement

Sizing Up Your Assets

Before you can start planning how to protect your
assets, you first have to make a full accounting
of exactly what they are. The following list can
help you make a start.

Market value of your home _____

Value of your furniture _____

Value of other items in your home _____

Estimated value of your car _____

Value of your investments _____

Value of your savings _____

Vested equity in company pension _____

Value of retirement investments _____

Cash value of life insurance _____

Other assets _____

value or the cash value. Getting replacement value coverage will cost a little more, but
this way if your home is destroyed you will be covered for the cost of replacing it
brick by brick. Replacement coverage also means that you don't have to worry if your
home appreciates in value over the years. Your coverage is complete whether your
home is worth $75,000 today or $100,000 in the future, excluding land.

Cash value coverage, on the other hand, merely extends to a flat dollar amount. You
can insure your home for $75,000, but if housing costs go up and replacing your

home ends up costing more than $75,000, the extra money will have to come out of your pocket. As you might expect, this type of coverage costs less than replacement value because the insurer is not taking as much of a financial risk to rebuild your home.

Another aspect of homeowner's insurance that's important to remember is the concept of liability. If people are injured on your property or you're sued for damages for an accident that occurred at your home or even far away, that's when the liability portion of insurance kicks in. You'll usually be required to have more liability coverage than the value of your home. That's basically to ensure that if you lose in a lawsuit and have to pay excessive damages, you won't also lose your house.

Not only are you protecting your home with homeowner's insurance, you're also protecting all the goodies that you have inside. (Antiques, jewelry, art, and the like might require a separate policy or rider.) That means you'll want to make sure that your uncle's antique ship clock and your grandmother's armoire are included in your coverage. As a general rule, your belongings are covered at about 50 to 70 percent of the value of your home. Also, if you have a cash value plan, you will be reimbursed only for what the item is worth today. So even if the great sentimental value of the armoire makes it priceless, you may find that its market value is just a few dollars.

The Different Types of Homeowner's Insurance

With rare exception, there are basically six different types of homeowner's insurance no matter what state you call home.

The first is called HO-1. This unromantic name for a plan covers just your basic needs. HO-1 covers your home and its valuables from fire or lightning, windstorm or hail, explosions, riots, aircraft, vehicles, smoke, vandalism, theft, damage by glass or safety glazing material that is part of a building, and last but not least, volcanic eruptions.

The second type of plan is called HO-2 (yes, there's a theme here). This plan gives you a little more coverage. On top of what you get from HO-1, HO-2 will cover you from falling objects, snow, electrical surge damage, water-related damage from home appliances, sonic booms, and damage from freezing pipes.

HO-3 gets even more fancy. Unless otherwise noted, HO-3 includes everything in the previous two plans plus protection for any additions you make to your house.

HO-4 and HO-6 plans are for renters and condo owners. Your coverage should under these plans include what you'd get with a combination of HO-1 and HO-2.

Owners of older homes should look into HO-8 coverage. This type of plan will protect you from damage caused by the 11 perils discussed with HO-1 coverage. HO-8 covers actual cash value, not rebuilding costs.

The cost of homeowner's insurance varies from region to region and from house to house. The average cost for a $125,000 home is somewhere around $450 a year. If you live in the Northeast you can expect to pay more. If you live in rural parts of the West, you'll probably pay less.

The law is on your side when it comes to finding a homeowner's policy. It's illegal for insurance companies to refuse you coverage based on your race, age, marital status, or gender. Your state's insurance department can help if you find yourself the victim of discrimination.

How Much Insurance Do You Need?

When you buy homeowner's insurance you don't necessarily have to go for a plan that has all the bells and whistles. For example, when deciding between a plan that has replacement value and a plan that has just cash value, you should ask yourself a few questions. If the home you're insuring is a second home or if you're not sure whether you would want to have the home rebuilt, then a cash value plan may make the most sense. Also you can expect to pay about 15 percent less on your policy if you go the cash value route.

If you're prepared to pay more for the security of knowing that come what may, you'll always have your home, then replacement coverage is your best bet. It's important to note, though, that if you opt for this plan, you will be required to rebuild the

home if it is destroyed. In contrast with a cash value plan the insurer simply cuts you a check and you can do whatever you wish with it.

Beware of falling into the trap of overinsuring your home and valuables. With replacement value insurance, for example, what you pay in premiums is based on the insurer's estimate of what your home is worth. If you believe the value is too high, you can always pay an appraiser to run the numbers again.

Floaters

You may find that many of the most valued treasures in your home are not covered by your standard homeowner's policy. In that case, you should look into separate coverage, usually called a "floater."

Floaters protect items that are lost, stolen, damaged, or destroyed in any conceivable way. What you pay for a floater is based on the value of the item you want covered, as well as where you live. Obviously, you will pay more if you live in Manhattan than if you live in Harrisburg, Virginia, or some other bucolic setting.

Make sure you have a good estimate of the value of the item you want floated. For items like jewelry and art, you'll want to go to an appraiser to get a price check. You can find out about appraisers in your area by contacting either the American Society of Appraisers (Box 17265, Washington, DC 20041, 800-272-8258) or the Appraisers Association of America (368 Park Avenue South, Suite 2000, New York, NY 10016, 212-889-5404). What you'll pay for an appraiser's services might be by the hour or by a prearranged fee.

It's also helpful to keep in mind that when you get a floater for an item, the coverage travels with that item. So you're protected whether your $3,000 wristwatch is damaged at home or stolen or lost on the other side of the globe.

It's a good idea to look into getting floaters for your more precious keepsakes. As you do an inventory of your belongings, you may find that there's more worth floating around than you might have imagined.

Resources to Tap for Answers to Your Insurance Questions

You may still have lots of questions concerning insurance, how to get it, what's covered, and what to do if there are problems. Luckily, there are several sources that can give you the answers.

Insurance Information Institute's Web page (HYPERLINK http://www.iii.org) can give you answers to many inquiries on car insurance and homeowner's policies.

FEMA, the Federal Emergency Management Agency, also has a solid Web site (HYPERLINK http://www.fema.gov). They can help you understand the ins and outs of when the government will step in to help with disaster relief and what steps you can take to help yourself after a natural disaster.

The Federal Trade Commission (HYPERLINK http://www.ftc.gov) can alert you to scams that you might not have thought about or prepared against. Remember, one person's disaster is another person's payday.

Home Insurance Shopping Tips

Let the free market be your best friend when it comes to shopping for homeowner's insurance. The insurance industry is quite competitive, and as a result you can reduce your premiums by as much as a few hundred dollars if you know where to look. The key is to call lots of insurers and do plenty of comparison shopping.

For an answer to the question "How do I choose an insurance company?" just call the National Insurance Consumer Helpline at (800) 942-4242. And if you click on to the

Insurance Information Institute's Web page (HYPERLINK http://www.iii.org), you can get loads of information on how to get the best deal for your insurance needs. You can also check out the reference section of your public library.

There are several ways to lower your premium. One way is to raise your deductible. Just as we saw with health insurance, if you raise your deductible, you lower costs for the insurer, and they in turn lower your premium. You can carry the health insurance analogy one step further. Nonsmokers tend to pay lower homeowner's insurance than the one-pack-a-day crowd. So stop smoking.

Another tip is to buy your home insurance, auto insurance, and other coverage from the same insurer. Many insurers will reward this one-stop shopping by giving you discounts of up to 15 percent. There's no secret why this strategy works, insurers want your business—all of it.

By making safety improvements inside your home and installing a home security system on the outside of your home you can entice your insurer to give you a premium cut. Some companies will lower what you pay by as much as 20 percent. Of course, you should make sure that all your improvements are cost-effective.

You should also make some calls to see if you can get group coverage. Your alma matter or one of the professional associations you're a member of may have a special discount package with an insurer. So ask around and see if you belong to an organization that can save you a bundle.

Renter's Insurance

If you're renting an apartment right now, you might not have thought about getting insurance for your belongings. After all, you might not have many valuables and there's probably some sort of security in your building. So why bother?

But if you walk around your one-bedroom and start listing the value of your furniture, stereo, computer, exercise equipment, and the like, you may find that getting renter's insurance makes a lot of sense. If disaster strikes, could you really afford to replace everything from scratch?

The basic insurance policy for renters, called HO-4, gives you coverage for loss as a result of fire or smoke, lightning, vandalism, theft, explosion, windstorm, and water damage from plumbing.

Just as with homeowner's insurance, renters have the choice of getting replacement coverage or cash value coverage. Interestingly, because renters tend to have less loot to protect, it costs less for renters to upgrade to replacement coverage than it does for homeowners to make the same choice. So if you want the extra peace of mind, it won't cost too much.

Renter's insurance also includes liability coverage, which is another good reason to consider it; everyone is at risk of being sued. And this coverage applies whether you're sued for actions that happened at your apartment or for something miles and miles away.

Car Insurance

It's important to remember that no matter how safe a driver you are, you're constantly at risk of being involved in an auto accident. This is true whether you live in a rural area or whether you commute every day along a major interstate highway.

Before you sit down to buy car insurance, it's wise to familiarize yourself with all the different types of coverage. Just as with health insurance and homeowner's insurance, you can't just walk into your insurer's office and say, "give me your regular plan." They vary state by state, except for two basic ones: bodily injury and property damage.

There are six parts to auto coverage: bodily injury liability, property damage liability, collision insurance, comprehensive insurance, medical payments coverage, and uninsured motorist's coverage. State law requires that you buy into some of these parts; other parts are up to your discretion.

Bodily injury liability covers you if you cause a car accident that kills or injures someone. Also, your court costs come with the coverage. There is no deductible, and all states require it. It's recommended that you buy coverage that exceeds what your state requires. So you should look into getting a plan that provides for $100,000

Protecting Your Money from the Effects of Divorce

If you have many assets to protect, then a prenuptial agreement may be a logical precaution to give you peace of mind.

Maintaining separate bank accounts may also make sense. After all, if you intermingle all your assets it may be very hard to separate out what's yours should you need to. Some states consider that the separate assets have been turned into marital assets. Also, if you have your money in a joint account, creditors may consider each of you responsible for any debts, even the ones that aren't your fault.

An individual account gives you your own financial freedom. It's the grown-up version of mad money. You should also consider keeping separate credit card accounts. Though it's important to remember, however, that all this freedom is not absolute. In community property states, like Arizona, California, Idaho, Louisiana, Nevada, New Mexico, Texas, Washington, and Wisconsin, you may still be responsible for debts that build up during your marriage.

Finally, a good way to prepare for your financial needs whether or not you get divorced is to maximize your contributions to your company's retirement plan. In the past many women counted on their husband's pension to protect them in their old age. But that type of thinking is ancient history. Although states now recognize pension and retirement plans to be marital assets, regardless of whose name they're in, you should float your pension so you have something to retire on, whether married or single.

worth of coverage for each person who gets injured and $300,000 worth of coverage per total accident. Otherwise you could find yourself with court cases and a lot of headaches.

Property damage liability is designed to protect you if you accidentally ruin someone else's property with your car. This property might be somebody's car or home. Just as with bodily injury coverage, your legal bills are paid for under a property liability plan. You've got to have *some* coverage, and it's recommended that you get at least $50,000 worth on each car that you have.

Collision insurance, as the name suggests, protects you if you find yourself in a collision with another car or even if you slam into a concrete barrier. Your coverage applies whether or not you are at fault. You'll have the choice of selecting a deductible for this type of coverage. Remember, just as with health insurance and homeowner's insurance, the higher the deductible you choose, the lower your premium will be. Since states do not require collision coverage, the decision is up to you and your comfort level. It makes more sense to get this optional insurance if your car is new and valuable.

Comprehensive insurance is also not mandated by the government. This variety of coverage expands your protection from perils such as fire, theft, falling objects, explosions, earthquakes, floods, and riots. If you have the extra money, this plan is good to have, just don't get more insurance than your car is actually worth.

Medical payments insurance deals with all the things we don't like to think about when we're on the road. If you suffered a long-term injury as a result of a car crash, medical payments coverage will chip in for your medical bills, lost wages from work, and your disability. This coverage protects you and your passengers, no matter who is at fault.

Uninsured motorist's coverage is a must, even though many states do not require it. The fact is that many people hop into their car and take to the roads every day without paying a dime in auto insurance. If one of these irresponsible drivers were to total your car, guess who would probably end up paying these bills? So get some uninsured motorist's coverage and thank yourself for the extra peace of mind. Just as with

bodily injury liability coverage, it is recommended that you get an uninsured motorist's plan that covers $100,000 for each person and $300,000 per accident.

It's also important to understand that some states have what is called a "no-fault" insurance system. That simply means that your insurer is required to make a payout for an accident whether or not you were at fault. In a "fault" state the insurer must pony up the money only if you can prove that you were not the cause of the accident. And it often requires a court case to sort those matters out.

Auto Insurance Shopping Tips

Just as with homeowner's insurance, it pays to make lots of phone calls and do comparison shopping. Start with the well-known insurers and ask what kind of coverage they offer and at what price. Never say yes to an offer after the first call. There may be another solid company that can offer you a better deal.

Also be sure to ask about special discounts. How much you pay for auto insurance is often based on your own unique situation. For example, if your car is extra safe (it has airbags, automatic seat belts, and an alarm system to deter theft), you can expect that your insurer will reward you with lower premiums.

If you spend only a little time on the road each year, your insurer would like to know. Because you don't fully expose yourself to the risks of the road, you are a cheaper bet to insure.

Insurance companies love safe drivers, and they put their money where their mouth is. If you have not gotten a ticket for the past few years you could get a premium discount. Also, young and older drivers who participate in driver training courses may be eligible for a premium cut.

And just as with a homeowner's plan, if you purchase all six parts of your auto coverage from the same insurer, you'll be rewarded with lower costs.

But don't stop there. You should be constantly reviewing your situation to see if you now qualify for extra discounts. For example, if your new job is so convenient to get

How Much Car Insurance Are You Required to Have?

It really depends on what state you call home. Your insurance agent can tell you what the minimums are. Note that there are three different minimums for car insurance: bodily injury per person, bodily injury per accident, and property damage.

In some states the minimum is quite high. Alaska, for example, requires $50,000 of coverage per person, $100,000 per accident, and $25,000 for property damage. Other states, such as Oklahoma, really don't mandate much coverage at all. The Sooner State asks only that you cover $10,000 per person, $20,000 per accident, and $10,000 for property damage.

Most states fall somewhere in the middle. The typical state will require coverage of, say, $25,000 to $30,000 per person, $40,000 to $50,000 per accident, and $15,000 to $20,000 for property damage.

Just remember that these are minimums, and you should always buy more coverage than the minimum. Otherwise you may find yourself paying for it later on.

to from home that you find yourself driving your car only a few thousand miles per year, then it's worth it to call your insurer to see if you can lower your premiums.

Liability and Umbrella Policies

As we saw earlier in this chapter, you need liability coverage to protect you from the vicissitudes of life. You could be sued for accidents that may or may not be your fault.

Leasing versus Buying a Car

Another vital question you have to consider concerning your car is whether to buy or lease the vehicle. Millions of people lease for many reasons. One of the most enticing is that they can often get a more expensive car with a lease. Of course, the downside is you don't own the car at the end of the lease.

Buying the car outright also has its advantages and disadvantages. On the plus side, you can keep the car as long as you wish. But then again, are you the sort of person who would keep on driving a car ten or even fifteen years after purchase?

If you decide to lease a car, you should be aware of the legal rights that are available to you. The Consumer Leasing Act seeks to set a level playing field as you go around and shop the best lease. Under the law, the car dealer must show you a breakdown of what is included in the lease, such as: the cost of the vehicle, the down payment, any trade-in allowance, the cost attributable to interest charges, the monthly payment, the residual value (what the car will be worth at the end of the lease), and all extra charges.

Some state laws may offer you additional rights when you lease. For information on these laws, contact your state's consumer protection agency or the attorney general's office. You also can contact:

Division of Consumer & Community Affairs
Mail Stop 800
Federal Reserve Board
Washington, DC 20551;

or

Consumer Response Center
Federal Trade Commission
6th and Pennsylvania Ave., NW
Washington, DC 20580

To get a copy of the informative "Keys to Vehicle Leasing" brochure,
call (202) 452-3244 or write to:

Publications Services, MS-127
Board of Governors of the Federal Reserve System
Washington, DC 20551

On the Web you can also click on to a helpful Federal Reserve site on
leasing (HYPERLINK http://www.bog.frb.fed.us/pubs/leasing/).

But if you're eventually held responsible for another party's injuries, that's when lia-bility protection kicks in. It's generally recommended that you obtain $300,000 to $500,000 of liability coverage.

Of course, how much you need depends on your circumstances. If you're single, with no dependents and living in an apartment, your liability needs are going to be dif-ferent from someone who is married with children and has a home, a pool, and a dog with an attitude. Also, if your home sits on lots of bare land that could be used or misused by friends or strangers, you're a prime candidate for extra liability protection.

Lately it has become fashionable to recommend so-called umbrella policies. They get that name because this type of protection is designed to give you maximum coverage that extends past your other insurance. If you get a $1 million umbrella policy, for example, coverage starts where your other insurance ends, say, after your $300,000 liability plan pays out.

Umbrella coverage covers two perils: 1) if you damage someone (either bodily or their property) due to your negligence; or 2) if you are unlucky enough to be victimized by someone who is uninsured or underinsured. Umbrellas also open up if you're sued for slander or defamation.

Just as with liability coverage, the size of your umbrella will depend on the life you lead and how much you have to protect. And remember, you can often save on premiums by buying your umbrella plan from the same company as your other insurance.

Insurance for Natural Disasters Like Floods

Unless you live by the ocean or near a major river, you probably think you don't need flood insurance. But floods can be caused by storms, hurricanes, or even melting snow. According to the Federal Emergency Management Agency, almost 30 percent of all flood insurance claims occur in low- to moderate-risk areas of the country.

Here's another reason to consider flood insurance: Flood damage is one of those perils that is not covered by your homeowner's policy. If the waters start to rise, guess who's going to pay?

If you decide to purchase flood insurance there are a few things to remember. Flood insurance is only offered by the federal National Flood Insurance Program. Although Uncle Sam is the one backing up the insurance, you can buy a policy from local agents at local private insurance companies. Note that you usually have to wait 30 days from the time of purchase before the policy takes effect, so think ahead of time.

You can buy flood insurance no matter where you live, as long as your community participates in the National Flood Insurance Program and is not in a designated Coastal Barrier Resources System area.

What you'll pay for flood coverage varies according to where you reside. If you live in a low-risk area, you might pay as little as $80 a year. The average premium is around $300 a year for $100,000 of coverage. You can insure your home for up to

Watch Out for Disaster Scammers

After a major disaster, whether it's a flood or a fire or an earthquake, you might find your home badly in need of repairs. Unfortunately, there are plenty of scam artists who use this opportunity to travel to your neighborhood and rip you off. So keep an eye out for the warning signs.

Watch out for builders and contractors who drop into your community, and go door-to-door, selling their wares. Always check to make sure they are licensed and that they can provide you with reference letters from satisfied customers. You can also ring up the Better Business Bureau to see if there have been any complaints filed with the builder or contractor.

Also, as you should with any major purchase, be sure to shop around and get several estimates. Don't allow yourself to be rushed into signing a contract until you're satisfied that you have the best deal.

If you still fall victim to a scammer, contact the consumer division of your state's attorney general's office.

$250,000 and its contents for up to $100,000. If you live in a flood plain, your lender will probably require flood insurance.

Q & A on What's Covered and Not Covered by Homeowner's Insurance

So far in this chapter we've talked about all sorts of insurance issues and what is covered and what is excluded. You can now take this little test to see if you've been

paying attention. You may even want to reread the chapter. And remember, no cheating!

Your best friend comes to visit but slips on your driveway and twists her ankle. Suddenly, she's not as friendly anymore. In fact, she sues you for damages. Are you covered? And how?

Your standard homeowner's policy will cover you for the legal bills from the resulting trial and will also chip in for whatever damages you end up paying.

You and your wife decide to spend a holiday with your grandparents. While your wife helps out with the dishes she accidentally loses her wedding ring down the drain. It's lost forever. Whose insurance will pay to replace it?

Mostly likely, nobody's plan covers this scenario. You'll have to buy a new ring completely from your own funds. This is why many people end up getting floaters for their more valuable items that are not covered by a standard homeowner's policy. Always read the fine print of your insurance contract to see what items are not covered.

What are "Acts of God" and am I covered for them?

You'll have to ask your priest, minister, or rabbi for an answer to the first part of that question, but as far as insurance coverage issues are concerned, this is the fully ordained answer: It really depends on the act. Floods are not covered by homeowner's plans, so you'll have to get some federal flood insurance. But as far as most other natural disasters, you should be covered under a standard homeowner's policy.

MONEY *for your heirs:* estate PLANNING

CHAPTER EIGHT

Estate planning is not just for the wealthy. As a matter of fact, it's even more important for people with limited means to plan carefully because the consequences of poor planning have more impact.

After all, when you have small amounts of money to play with, every little bit counts. Fortunately, new tax laws are on your side. The traditional $600,000 of your estate that you used to be able to pass along tax-free will now increase annually, until the cap reaches $1 million in the year 2006. For some estates, the top rate is 60 percent, but that is very rare. This chapter outlines the structure you need to set up to be sure that government regulations and the IRS don't eat up your money when you die before your loved ones get it.

Life Insurance

Life insurance provides an income for your family when you die. Don't wait to purchase life insurance, because as hard as it is to think about death, it could happen at any time. And when that day comes, your family will have to deal with expenses as well as grief. Who will pay your unpaid bills? Who will supplement the salary that won't be coming in? Who will pay for the funeral? That's where life insurance comes in. Learn about the different types of life insurance and how much you need.

Life insurance can also be used as a financial tool to help you pay for retirement or college. But it's wise to focus on life insurance as a death benefit and not an investment vehicle. See chapter 3 for information and advice on investment strategies.

How much life insurance you need basically depends on how much of a financial loss you would be if you died. That's a horrible thing to have to think about, but it really is that simple. If you're single, with no dependents and no attachments, then your life insurance needs will be slight. You will leave no financial hole that needs to be filled. But say you're married with a few kids, a mortgage, car payments, and to top it all off you're the sole wage earner in the family. Your death would be financially devastating to many people. In this case, life insurance is a must.

The Different Flavors of Life Insurance

Just as with health insurance, homeowner's insurance, and every other insurance you can think of, life insurance does not come in a one-size-fits-all box. There is a wide variety of life insurance products to choose from, so take time to familiarize yourself with them.

Term insurance is the most basic. The most bang for the buck. It gives you protection for a specified period of time, and if you die during that time (or term, hence the name) the policy pays out a benefit. The term can be for 1 year or for 20 years, and the coverage can be a few thousand dollars or hundreds of thousands of dollars. For example, if you buy a ten-year term policy worth $200,000, and you die within that ten-year period, your beneficiaries will collect the $200,000.

The advantages to term life insurance include the fact that the simplicity of the policy also means your premiums will generally be lower than for other more complicated life insurance products. Also, because you can pick a policy that has a long term or a short term, you have the flexibility to cover whatever specific (and maybe temporary) needs your family may face, such as paying off a mortgage or a car loan.

The downside to a term policy is that once your specified term is done, so is your insurance. You may be able to renew the policy, but then again, the premiums at that point may be too expensive to continue.

There is another class of life insurance vehicles that go under the title of "permanent insurance." These life insurance products include whole life plans, variable life plans, and universal life plans.

Most permanent insurance policies include a feature known as "cash value" or "cash surrender value," which gives you the choice to cancel your policy while you're still kicking and get the cash value of the plan in a lump sum. Of course, if you do this too early there may be very little cash value to take out. Another feature of cash surrender value allows you to skip premiums as long as you then use the cash value of your policy to continue your coverage. Finally, cash value plans may let you borrow from your insurance company by using the cash value in your policy as collateral.

As you might guess from the name, whole life policies are designed to cover you for your whole life, not just a specified term. You don't have to renew the plan every couple of years, and the premiums you pay generally stay constant over the life of the policy.

Universal life insurance gives you a lot of flexibility. Within certain constraints you are allowed to vary how much you pay in premiums as well as when you pay. Also, the level of death benefit can be adjusted. If you suddenly want to ratchet up your death benefit, though, you'll usually have to confirm that your health is still good.

Variable life is a life insurance plan for people who are comfortable with making their own investment decisions. This type of policy lets you choose how to invest your premiums among stocks, bonds, or a combination. If you choose wisely, your benefits can grow quite large. But the cash value of this type of plan is not guaranteed. Just as we saw in chapter 3, the concept of risk versus reward is very much at work here.

Some variable plans give you a safety net by guaranteeing that death benefits will not fall below a certain minimum amount.

The advantages and disadvantages to permanent insurance are varied and depend on your needs. On the plus side, your premiums can be fixed or flexible to be custom-fit to your financial situation. You can borrow against the plan, or get the money while you're still alive. And your coverage can be guaranteed for life. But all these options can come with a high price tag, and you may find it difficult to purchase enough coverage.

Life insurance trusts are still another way to play the life insurance game. This type of trust lets your proceeds pass directly to your beneficiaries without having to go through the process of probate. Life insurance proceeds paid to a named beneficiary will also avoid probates. We'll talk more about probate later in this chapter. The proceeds from a life insurance trust are administered by a trustee for your beneficiaries. Irrevocable life insurance trusts also let you avoid taxes when you die. The catch is that unlike with other life insurance, you don't own an irrevocable life insurance trust, and you don't have control over the plan.

Shopping for Life Insurance

More than 1,500 companies in the United States sell life insurance. So how to choose? It's always helpful to check around with your friends and family to see where they get their insurance and if they are satisfied. You'll also need to look into your prospective insurer's financial stability and credentials.

You can contact your state's insurance department to make sure the firm is licensed in your state, and you can walk over to your local library (the bigger the better) to get books that rate the financial strength of insurers. You can also go online to check out the rating services, like A. M. Best (HYPERLINK http://www.ambest.com) and Weiss Ratings (HYPERLINK http://www.weissratings.com).

One good way to see what the going rate is for term insurance is to call or click on to an insurance quote service. These firms are like travel agents for life insurance. All you have to do is tell them a little about yourself and what kind of insurance you're looking for and they will list for you what they believe are the best rates you can get. They are a free service to you, but remember that they make their money by getting a commission on the policies they sell. Two of these services are QuickQuote, (800) 867-2404 (HYPERLINK http://www.quickquote.com), and Quotesmith (800) 431-1147 (HYPERLINK http://www.quotesmith.com).

You can buy life insurance directly from a company or you can enlist the help of an agent. If you choose an agent, make sure that he or she is licensed to sell life insurance. All states require this. And if the agent sells variable insurance policies that person must be registered with the National Association of Securities Dealers. Your agent may also have a professional designation, such as Chartered Life Underwriter (CLU) or Life Underwriter Training Council Fellow (LUTCF).

An agent will sit you down and discuss your life insurance needs and questions. The agent will also ask you detailed questions about your family income, net worth, health, personal habits, mental condition—the works. So be ready to answer. From this debriefing the agent will then have a good idea of what type of insurance is in your best interest and at what cost.

Before you put your money down and buy a policy, check to make sure you have a grace period, or "free look period," during which you can change your mind. You'll usually only get only about ten days (it varies state by state), so during that time be sure to read all the fine print in your contract to make sure there are no errors and that the policy is what you really need. If you decide to cancel, the insurer will give you an appropriate refund. Ask your agent beforehand how this will work.

Wills

A will makes sure your belongings and your money go to the people you want to get them. A will is a legal document that dictates your financial and personal wishes after you're gone. Financially, a will basically lays out who gets what. Who will get the jewelry, the furniture, the car, and the coin collection? Just put it in your will. And when it comes to your personal affairs, a will can let your survivors know who you want to look after your children and other dependents.

Legal Help

You can make your will out by yourself, but to be on the safe side, it makes sense to consult with an attorney. Remember, this is a legal document that we're talking about, and one slip-up on your part may cause the will to be invalidated. The language you use in the will may be too vague or you may forget some items that you wanted to include.

Lawyers do wills all the time, so they have the experience to know what's important and not important to have in your will. If you've used an attorney in the past, you may be able to work with that person on your will or ask him or her to recommend someone else. The local branch of the bar association can provide names and advice as well. Financial planners also often take care of these matters. If your estate is complicated by many assets and many people trying to get their hands on those assets then you should look for a lawyer who specializes in estate planning.

One organization that can help you find an estate planning attorney is the American College of Trust and Estate Counsel. For a list of lawyers in your area, just click on to their Web site (HYPERLINK http://www.actec.org).

What you pay for legal services may be a flat fee or an hourly rate. Depending on the size and complexity of your estate, you may end up forking over a few hundred dollars or a few thousand dollars. But the peace of mind may well be worth it.

legal jargon, this is called dying "intestate." If you die intestate it's then up to the courts to make the big decisions you should have made in your will. And you may not like the choices the court makes. States have standard formulas that they use to parcel out property. Wouldn't you rather have a say?

That said, it's important to remember that not all your property needs to go through a will. In fact, a lot of your money is already predetermined to go to whom you want it to. This includes the cash you have in an Individual Retirement Account (IRA), a life insurance policy, and your company's pension plan, as long as you have named a beneficiary. Also, assets that you and your spouse own jointly, such as a bank account, will pass to your surviving spouse with no will and no problem.

So what goes in a will? Here's a rundown:

- Your name and address, as well as the names of your spouse, kids, and anyone you want to be beneficiaries in your will

- A list of your assets, along with specifics as to who gets what

- A list of alternate beneficiaries in case a beneficiary dies before you do

- Establishment of a trust (we'll explain trusts later in this chapter)

- The name of your "executor," who will take care of your wishes and personal effects when you pass away. Your executor pays off your creditors, as well as Uncle Sam, and notifies Social Security and other agencies that you have passed. Other mundane but necessary duties include canceling your credit cards. You can choose your spouse, an adult child, another relative, or an attorney—anyone you trust who is over 18, a U.S. citizen, (and not a convicted felon)—to be your executor.

- Possibly the name of a "guardian," who will take care of your minor children. Although the surviving parent usually becomes the guardian, it's still important to name one in your will in case neither you nor your spouse is able or willing to step in.

You'll then need to sign the will and get witnesses for certification. The document should also be notarized.

DO-IT-YOURSELF FORMS AND SOFTWARE FOR YOUR WILL

If you decide to draw up your will on your own, be sure to do a lot of research. Your local library should have books on will preparation. Also, a trip to your local computer superstore will help you uncover the numerous software packages that are designed for good will writing.

You can go the high-tech route, but don't bother writing your will out in your own hand. Not all states consider these documents to be valid wills, and you don't need the hassle of maybe creating a document that may not do what you want it to.

The Problems of Probate

Probate is the legal procedure that governs how your estate is distributed. One of the first things your executor has to do after you die is to file your will with probate court, which then determines whether or not the will is valid. Once that hurdle is crossed, your assets are distributed.

Along the way, though, the probate process can take months to work out and may cost as much as 10 percent of the assets in your estate. It's also important to remember that wills that pass through probate are public documents, so anyone can find out how much loot you left behind.

Not all assets have to show up in probate. As mentioned earlier in this chapter, what you have tied up in IRAs, pensions, and life insurance plans will go directly to your named beneficiary. Also, jointly held property gets to slip between probate's cracks. And assets held in a living trust pass to named beneficiaries without going through the probate process.

Estate Taxes

It seems that taxes follow you wherever you go. Buy a home, a car, or even a stick of bubble gum, and you pay taxes. And for some Americans, the IRS follows you even into the grave.

Federal estate taxes are generally due if your net taxable estate is worth more than $625,000. But that number is not set in stone. The number will index up from 1998 to 2006 and will eventually include $1,000,000 of your estate. If you're subject to

the federal tax expect to see rates start at 37 percent and go as high as 55 percent.

You might think that there's no way your estate is worth anything near $625,000. But you'd be surprised how quickly your assets can add up. A partial list might include your home, car, furniture, artwork, stocks, bonds, and retirement assets. And once Uncle Sam has taken his share, you then have to worry about your state's death or inheritance taxes.

There are ways to lessen the size of your estate taxes. As you're about to see in this chapter, you can establish a trust or gift your money away during your lifetime. You can also cover the costs associated with estate taxes by buying a life insurance policy that is designed to pay taxes. Your life insurance agent or attorney can show you how to set one up.

Unlimited Marital Deduction

One easy way to avoid paying any estate taxes when you die is to make use of the unlimited marital deduction. And it really is unlimited. Whether your estate is under $625,000 or over $6,000,000, the marital deduction lets you just transfer everything over to your sweetheart.

That may be the easy way for you, but it might not be the best long-term choice. Giving all your property to your spouse may just delay the inevitable. While your spouse will not have to deal

HOUSEKEEPING AND YOUR WILL

Because your will is so vital to your overall estate planning strategy, it's important to make several copies. You can then distribute your will to the people who will be the most important in carrying out your wishes. Copies can go to your executor and your guardian. You can also tell close friends and relatives where you have kept copies. If you used the services of a lawyer to draw up your will, that person can keep the original, or you can give him or her a copy with a note explaining where the original is located.

You may want to stash your will in a safe-deposit box. That provides a certain amount of safety, though you should know that some states seal your safe-deposit box after you die. This action may result in a delay in carrying out the instructions in your will.

with taxes if he or she remarries after you pass away the fact is your spouse may not live much longer than you do. And once your spouse dies, Uncle Sam swoops in to collect estate taxes. If your estate is grand enough to qualify for the tax, then it's your children or other beneficiary that will pay for your lack of planning.

Another way to have your estate avoid taxation is to give it away to charity upon your death. So if you really believe in a cause, you might want to contact that charity. They'll definitely be happy to answer all your questions.

You can also use the marital deduction or charity deduction in a more limited and strategic form if your goal is merely to reduce the value of your estate so that your property is taxed at a lower rate.

Joint Accounts

It makes a lot of sense to name a relative, such as your spouse or your child, as being joint on your accounts. And most of your assets, such as your checking or savings account, as well as your mutual funds, can be set up in joint accounts.

Having your assets in joint accounts enables your heirs to gain access to funds easily to write checks to cover debts and free up cash. This strategy also facilitates your spouse's access to funds in the event of a disabling illness. Moreover, setting up joint accounts enables your children to gain access to funds to take care of incapacitated parents. Of course, you need to make sure that you have the requisite amount of trust in this person to give him or her access to your savings.

Property that is jointly held with the right of survivorship doesn't pass through probate; it simply passes to the survivor. This can be your spouse or another person who is close to you. It's important to remember, though, that you then can't redirect this property to someone else in your will.

Giving It Away before You Go

The way the government sees things, it's better to give than to receive. Of course, this maxim applies more to you than to them.

Under the law you can give your money away tax-free to anyone and everyone you wish. This financial tactic makes sense if your estate is large, because each gift you make reduces the size of your estate and thus reduces the chance that you'll be hit with estate taxes when you die. And even if your estate does end up paying taxes, the rate of taxation should be less because your estate has shrunk due to all the gifts.

The annual exclusion enables you to give up to $10,000 ($20,000 for married couples) per year to anyone: relatives, friends, even your doorman. Not only do you not pay any taxes, neither does the lucky recipient of your largess.

The power of this tool should not be overlooked, especially later in life. Say you're married with two children who are themselves married. That means you and your wife can make gifts totaling up to $80,000 tax free in any given year. And after 1998, the $10,000-per-person limit will rise and be indexed for inflation.

Gifts to Minors

Parents or grandparents who want to transfer assets over to the next generation can benefit from two important tax laws. Under the Uniform Transfers to Minors Act (UTMA), you can take any property you may have, ranging from real estate to stocks, to cash, and set up an account for your child or grandchild. You can do this at a bank or with your broker. You then name a custodian to control the account until the minor is a minor no more. That might be age 18 or 21, depending on where you live.

These UTMA accounts have a nice tax advantage. For the first $650 of earnings in the account, the tax rate is 0 percent. Not bad. For the next $650, the rate is the child's tax rate, which is most likely 15 percent. Anything over $1,300 is taxed at the parent's marginal rate.

Under the Uniform Gift to Minors Act (UGMA), your choice of asset is more limited. With the UGMA you can put, for example, mutual funds or bank deposits into an account that is controlled by a custodian. You can name yourself as the custodian, though if you do, the account will be considered as part of your estate when you die.

The downside to the UGMA and the UTMA is that once your child hits age 18 or 21, he or she gets the money outright. If you want to have more control over your gift, you should consider transferring the assets to a children's trust, such as a so-called Crummey trust. This kind of trust lets the trustee control the money as long as he or she wants. It also gives kids the right to withdraw the amount of your gift each year.

Trusts: An Introduction

A trust is a legal arrangement that enables an individual, called a grantor, to hold property for another person or a group of other people. The assets fall under the control of a trustee, who manages and distributes the assets according to the wishes of the grantor.

Setting up a trust is kind of like preparing a will. You have to detail your wishes, name beneficiaries, and designate a trustee to manage the assets. Also, some states require that you document your trust by filing papers with the state.

Be sure you have faith in the person you pick as your trustee. This person will be the one who invests the cash or manages the property you have in the trust. If you want professional help, a bank or an attorney can be selected as trustee. Of course, that means you'll have to pay them a small fee, say 1 percent to 2 percent of the trust's assets. These details should be worked out in advance.

You could also select a relative or close friend who has financial expertise as your trustee. The rates will be more reasonable, and you may feel more comfortable dealing with someone who understands you, your wishes, and your risk tolerance when it comes to the management of your assets. Either way, it's important to understand that a trustee's first obligation is to look out for the best interests of the beneficiaries when managing the trust.

Trusts can be broken down into two groups: afterdeath trusts and living trusts. Afterdeath trusts, also called "testamentary" trusts, take effect upon your death. This type of trust will pass through the probate process if the assets in the trust are not given out to a trustee during your lifetime.

Living trusts, also called "inter vivos" trusts, implement your wishes while you're still alive. For example, a parent could set up a trust where the profits or income from the assets go to a child, but the child does not own the property or other asset. We'll have more to say about living trusts later in this chapter.

Advantages and Disadvantages of Trusts

Trusts are not just for the richest of the rich. In fact, many people in different financial situations can benefit from a trust. There are several key advantages to setting up and maintaining a trust. First, trusts enable you to give your heirs money while still maintaining some control over how it's used.

Also, you can use a trust to disburse assets to minor children, dependents, or other family members who just don't have enough financial savvy to manage the assets on their own. Trusts can also be used to manage your own assets should you ever become unable to take care of your finances yourself.

One of the big pluses of trusts is that the assets they contain avoid probate. What you have in trusts is private and not a matter of public record. Trusts can also reduce or otherwise provide for payment of estate taxes. Finally, trusts may be flexible and, depending on the kind of trust, may be changed at any time.

But trusts are not for everyone. Legal fees to set up a trust can be quite high, anywhere from, say, $600 to even $20,000. (There are inexpensive computer programs, such as Quicken Family Lawyers, that can help you prepare your own trust documents.) And maintaining a trust requires ongoing planning. Also, a trust might be improperly drafted or misinterpreted, and it might be challenged by your heirs. And divorce does not revoke a former spouse's interest in some trusts.

Finally, a well-written will may be just as effective in distributing your assets as a trust. And wills tend to be cheaper to set up than trusts. So check with a lawyer before making up your mind.

Living Trusts

Among the different flavors of trusts are living trusts. They can be "revocable" or "irrevocable" depending on your needs. Revocable trusts are more popular, as they allow you the flexibility to make changes to the trust. Although they let you avoid probate, revocable trusts are not sheltered from federal or state estate taxes.

An irrevocable trust is set in stone. Once you draw it up and name your beneficiary there's no going back. As far as the tax law is concerned, this type of trust is a separate entity from you. You cannot take the money out and the grantor (that's you) is bound by the arrangements under which you set it up. In return for these draconian rules, the assets contained in the irrevocable trust get reduced tax treatment on estate taxes. Plus, you get to avoid probate.

Grantor-Retained Interest Trusts

We are now about to enter the alphabet soup of estate planning trusts. Don't let all the acronyms get you down, just stay focused on what each type of trust can offer you.

There are a variety of grantor-retained interest trusts (also know as GRITs). Some GRITs deal with securities, others with real estate. Some are used to help relatives, others are used to benefit people outside your family. But they all offer the same tax advantage: the ability to lock in the item's tax basis now, when the value of the item is lower than it will be after you're gone.

One type of GRIT is a qualified personal residence trust (also called as QPRT). This is one option to think about if you have an expensive home that you don't want to include in your estate, but you still want to live there. What you do is set up a time period, say 20 years, that you and your spouse will occupy the home; after that the house goes to your child. By making this generous gift to your child, you have reduced how much tax will be due. A QPRT enables you to transfer ownership of your house to your heirs tax-free.

But the fine print of this deal may exclude you from wanting to make this choice. Once the 20 years is up, you have to start paying rent to your kids for the right to stay in the home. And the rent can't be a symbolic $1 a month; it has to be market based. Also, the trust dissolves if you die before the set time limit is reached, and that puts the home back in your estate.

If you'd rather give your home to a charity than to your kids, you might want to consider a life estate agreement. This option is not a GRIT or a QPRT, but it may serve your purposes if you want to be socially responsible and if your children wouldn't want or need the house anyway. A life estate agreement signs away your home to the charity of your choice, although you are still allowed to live there for the rest of your life. Upon your death, the charity gets the house.

Charitable Remainder Trusts

This flavor of trust lets you bequeath your assets to charity while at the same time enabling you to take a tax deduction on the property's value. And as an added bonus, you can receive payments based on the value of the donated assets.

Two types of charitable remainder trusts are CRUTs and NIMCRUTs. With a charitable remainder unitrust (or CRUT), the payments you get are fixed every year, based on the trust's annually recalculated total value. With a net income with makeup provision charitable remainder trust (you guessed it, NIMCRUT), you have more flexibility. A NIMCRUT allows you to defer your annual payments as your investment grows tax-free. Then when you need the income, say when you retire, you can make up for lost time by taking higher payouts.

Charities may also have what are called "pooled income funds." Here your assets are intermingled (or pooled) with the donations of other charitable souls. The income you earn is then based on what the fund earns each year. Management of the fund might be by the charity or by an outside financial expert. The tax break to you might

be 25 percent to 50 percent of your donation, depending on your age and what the fund makes.

Charitable Gift Annuities

The charity works both ways with a charitable gift annuity. This annuity lets you combine your generous nature with a desire for fixed income. Charitable gift annuities are generally designed for older, more conservative investors.

Here's how it works: You donate, say $10,000, to a deserving cause and in return you receive a fixed income payment for the rest of your life, not tax-free, but tax-reduced. Now what you'll receive is not much, maybe a few hundred dollars a year, but charitable gift annuities are just one tool that major charities such as the American Red Cross or the American Heart Association are using to entice more donors.

Charitable Trust with Insurance

You can also use your life insurance policy to help out both a deserving cause and your heirs. With a charitable trust with insurance, you set up a charitable remainder trust and a life insurance policy. The value of the policy will be the same as the value of the assets you've put into the trust. After you pass away the charity gets the trust's money, but the insurance policy pays off to the insurance trust, which will then pay off to your heirs, and the tax bite will be less than if you had given the heirs the money outright. You can also set up a life insurance trust that will exempt death benefits from estate taxes.

Charitable Lead Trust

This trust is different from charitable remainder trusts. With a charitable lead trust, you donate assets, such as from the sale of stock, to a qualified worthy cause. The charity then receives the income from the account as long as you're alive, or for whatever time period you specify. After that, the assets are turned over to your heirs.

The longer the charity keeps these assets, the greater the tax break will be when your heirs take over. In addition, if the trust's return on the investment is greater than anticipated, the excess goes to your heirs without tax.

Q-tips

No, these Q-tips don't go in your ears. This acronym stands for qualified terminal interest property trusts. What a Q-tip does is let your financial wishes continue long after you and your spouse have passed away.

Q-tips let you pass an unlimited amount of money to your spouse without your estate taking a tax hit. This, of course, sounds a lot like the unlimited marital deduction that we talked about earlier in this chapter. But there's a twist. With the standard marital deduction your spouse, say your wife, gets total control of the money when you die. She can do whatever she wishes with the assets, and upon her death can then give the remaining assets to whomever she wishes. With a Q-tip, you get to say what happens to the remaining money after your spouse dies.

WHAT DOESN'T BELONG IN A TRUST

Although trusts are valuable for many of your estate planning goals, you need to be selective when you choose the assets that you fill them with.

You also have to be aware of the tax implications. For example, IRAs, 401(k)s, and other similar tax-deferred retirement plans do not belong in a trust. If you were to move an IRA or 401(k) into a trust, you would then have to pay all the taxes due, because you are taking it out of its shelter.

This distinction is important, for example, if you're on your second marriage. A Q-tip will provide lifelong support to wife number two, and after her death you can arrange it so that the remaining principal from the trust goes to the children from your first marriage.

Grantor-Retained Annuity Trusts

This trust, called a GRAT, is used for business needs and for transferring company stock while reducing taxes. Here's one example of how it can work: say you have stock in your company that you've held for decades, and you want to shift some of it over to your daughter. If the stock has jumped in value over the years, which would not be surprising, an outright transfer of the stock could really be hit with taxes.

But if you set up a GRAT, the gift is sheltered from taxes somewhat because you retain the right to receive annual payments from the assets in the trust. And you can do this for a set number of years, say ten years. After that, the assets in the trust go to your beneficiary—in this case, your daughter.

Because you're funneling income from the trust, the gift that your daughter gets is considered less valuable by the IRS than if you had just opened up your wallet. The math is calculated like this: Take the fair market value of the assets at the time of the gift—say, $100,000—and subtract the present value of the income that you will get over the ten years (in this example) of the trust—say, $20,000. What remains is eligible for gift taxes.

The catch to this strategy is similar to the caveat for the QPRT. If you die before the term of the trust is completed, the assets are sent back to your estate.

YOUR *money* Online

CHAPTER NINE
What we know as the Internet has actually been around for approximately three decades, yet nobody outside the government or the academic world used it until about ten years ago. In that short time, it has become ubiquitous.

We search for information, we talk to friends and family, and some of us even do a little commerce with our computer. But is it safe? What are the risks? And what precautions should you take to guard your privacy and your money?

What Are the Risks When Surfing?

Where to begin? Well, for starters, your identity can be stolen, your privacy can be infringed upon, viruses can destroy your valued data, and scam artists can use the Net to separate you from your cash.

Hackers are famous for digging into personal information that is stored in comput-

ers. Data such as your Social Security and checking account numbers can be hacked and have been hacked from government and corporate computer databases, and even your home PC. In fact, a recent presidential commission on computer security concluded that federal and state officials are not prepared to deal with the threats to our electronic infrastructure. And that infrastructure is growing increasingly more vulnerable as more and more people conduct their daily personal and business activities over the Internet.

Even your personal medical information can be lifted. When U.S. Representative Nydia Velazquez ran for office in 1993, her hospital records (which detailed an attempted suicide years before) were downloaded and sent to the media.

Moreover, you don't have to be acting illegally to get information on somebody's personal finances. There are several pay services, acting totally within the law, that use the information floating around in cyberspace to construct a profile of your buying and spending habits, the value of big ticket items like your home, and even the intimate details of an inheritance or divorce.

Spammers

If you're like most people, your mailbox is routinely stuffed with junk mail. This mail might include stacks of catalogs, free offers for products you don't want or need, and maybe requests for money in get-rich-quick schemes.

The computer version of this is "spam" mail. Spammers send unsolicited commercial e-mail to unwilling Internet users, which costs the recipient both time and sometimes money. Spamming is becoming a growing problem as more and more people get e-mail access. The size of the audience is now just too large for direct mailers to ignore.

So watch out if you see messages that pop up saying "your e-mail address was obtained from a reputable source," or "remove the top name from the list, add yours at the bottom," or "call 1-900-xxx-xxxx."

You can also check out HYPERLINK (http://www.junkbusters.com). This site will show you how to track down spammers and send them a strongly worded letter to make them cease and desist.

Real-Life Examples of Cyber-Fraud

Before we focus on the negative, it's important to remember that the Internet is a valuable asset; it's a great aid in research and can even help you perform the daily tasks of life. You can obtain quotes on your favorite stock, book airline tickets to Jamaica, and chat with your best friend in London all at the click of your mouse.

You can also get all sorts of advice over the Net. And that's where much of the risk of the Internet comes in. One of the more frightening examples of how Internet advice giving can go awry deals with medical information and the search for "cures."

In Sioux City, Iowa, for example, a 60-year-old woman died and another was hospitalized after drinking a "medicinal" tea that they found being hyped on the Internet. In other cases, ads for experimental drugs and other concoctions are placed in online newsgroups by marketing companies who cloak the ads as testimonials. The ad might go something like this: "My daughter has had asthma since before she could walk. Our doctor prescribed several drugs that all had harmful side effects. I had lost all hope until I found (fill in the name of the drug). Now she hasn't had an attack in three years."

There are several problems here and they all involve issues like objectivity, verifiability, and plain common sense. First off, how can you be sure the advice you're getting is unprejudiced? All you have to go on are words typed up on a computer screen. Who's standing behind those words: a doctor, a pharmaceutical company, the *New England Journal of Medicine*, or a New Age shaman? If the concoction you choose to use is merely a face cream, then maybe who cares? You're only out five or ten bucks, and at worst you'll feel a little silly. But if the medical product you're experimenting with is more serious, the answer could mean the difference between life and death.

Verification is vital. Check out the credentials of anyone making medical claims on the Net. Better still, ask your doctor if she has heard of product X and what her opinion is. Also ask for a rundown of some reputable medical sites on the Web. If you're getting positive feedback about a treatment from your doctor as well as from several reliable medical sites, then you can feel more at ease.

And as we saw in chapter 6, there are many Web sites that dispense solid medical

information. There are government sites such as the one from the Centers for Disease Control, and nonprofit Web pages from the American Lung Association and American Heart Association. Also, well-established medical centers like Johns Hopkins and the Mayo Clinic can be of value.

The problem is that it's so easy to run into faulty information. Newsgroups seem to be a breeding ground for medical snake-oil salesmen. All you have to do is go to a large search engine and type in the word of most any ailment, say arthritis or cancer. What you'll find will be a list of hits for medical quackery mixed in with hits for reputable information from medical journals. Sorting out which is which can take a keen eye and a lot of time.

If you want to stay abreast of what sites to be wary of, you can click to a site called Quackwatch (HYPERLINK http://www.quackwatch.com). It's run as a non-profit by Dr. Stephen Barrett, who is an author on questionable medical data. His Web pages display a hall of shame for medical advice. There are examples of questionable medical advertisements and doctor sites, as well as tips on how to spot quacks and how to avoid being quacked. He also gives links to other quack watchers.

Cyber-Risks to Internet Stock Trading

Conducting business over the Web is now done millions of times a day. And one area of commerce that holds the most promise as a growth industry is the online buying and selling of stocks.

In many ways, the Internet is ideal for trading securities. The Web can be your broker by giving you access to the kinds of research and advice that previously were found only in large brokerage houses. The Web can act as an investment bank by attracting investors to put their capital into a company. The Web can even act as a market, bringing together buyers and sellers under one cyber-roof. And by eliminating all these middlemen, the Net can lower the costs of trading and save you a bundle.

But just as with medical fraud, there are many financial quacks in cyberspace. In this case you might not lose your life, but you may lose your life savings.

Instead of peddling a silver-bullet drug to cure, say, baldness, the financial scamster touts the stock of a company that is peddling a silver-bullet cure for baldness. Let's call the company Bald-a-Way. Before the "miracle" drug can be proven a fake by government regulators like the Food and Drug Administration, the purveyors of Bald-a-Way can still make a lot of cash.

Here's how they do it: The company sets up a fancy-looking Web page that it fills to the brim with (phony) medical reports on the drug's efficacy and message postings on the drug and its growth potential. Also, the site includes information on how to get in on the ground floor of this buying opportunity. Spam mail (with links to the Bald-a-Way home page) is then distributed to millions of unsuspecting online stock traders hyping the stock, and stealth ads for the stock suddenly pop up in financial newsgroups masked as testimonials from "real-life" users of the drug. The buzz builds, the stock's price gets driven up, and the scam artists cash out before the bubble bursts. Those who don't sell quickly, lose everything.

These types of Net scams work best with thinly traded stocks. Although tiny companies can have the greatest growth potential, it's often next to impossible to get independent analysis of their business practices and financial prospects. Brokerages probably don't cover them, and regulators may not give these small fry enough scrutiny. And because of the limited number of buyers and sellers, you may not be able to find a seller when you need to.

If you run afoul of these financial Web scams, the Securities and Exchange Commission would like to hear from you. They regulate both the securities you can hold in your hand and the ones floating in cyberspace. Their e-mail address is HYPERLINK mailto:enforcement@sec.gov.

The Year 2000 Problem

This crisis (often called the Y2K problem) is all too real, and yet few people seem to care. To save space, most computer systems were designed to represent a year as two digits. For example, "1998" to a computer is just "98." But when we reach the year 2000, many computers will see "00" and incorrectly assume it's the year 1900.

INVASION OF THE IDENTITY SNATCHERS

Armed with your personal information, a crook can assume your identity in a financial sense. All thieves need are your name, address, and credit card number to start their shopping spree. And if they get their hands on your Social Security number and brokerage account number, crooks can tiptoe through your investments, make trades, and even cash in. In 1995 the FBI arrested one hacker who had 30,000 credit card numbers that were pilfered from a California Internet provider.

For more information on what's at stake and what action to take, you can contact the Privacy Rights Clearinghouse at: 1717 Kettner Ave., Suite 105, San Diego, CA 92101, (619) 298-3396. You can also click on to their Web site (HYPERLINK http://www.privacyrights.org) or get their book *The Privacy Rights Handbook* (Avon, 1997).

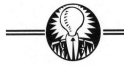

This arcane computer glitch could set up a financial domino effect where bills don't get paid on time, your ATM doesn't spit out the cash you request, and buy and sell orders for securities are not executed. And there doesn't seem to be any easy fix. Solving the problem for many old mainframes means ripping out the old computer code line by line.

Many companies are spending big bucks to renovate their systems. If you're worried that your money might be at risk, now is the time to contact your bank, brokerage, mutual fund, or other institution that is computer dependent and ask them a few questions. For starters, ask if they have done a comprehensive review of their computer system to see how vulnerable they are. Then find out what their timetable is to test and green-light their new system.

You can also ask them what would happen if you wanted to make a withdrawal or sell stock in December 1999 or early January 2000 and the company or a company that they're dealing with is having computer problems and your withdrawal or sale is delayed. What would the company then do for you?

The government, whose aging computers don't stand a chance against the year 2000 meltdown, is beginning to take notice. They're revamping their systems and also lending a hand to the private sector. Congress recently passed legislation that directs federal banking agencies and the National Credit Union Administration Board to give seminars to banks and credit unions on how to test and fix their computer networks.

Luckily, your personal computer and the software you load it up with should be able to weather the storm. Microsoft's Windows, as well as other operating systems, will be unaffected because they use all four digits to represent a year.

Passwords and Encryption Technology

One of the keys to cyber-safety is choosing a password that is hard to crack. If thieves were to find your password (or guess what it is), they could be just as damaging as if they had stolen your Social Security number or brokerage account number. Remember, in the cyber world where nobody sees your face, your personal identification numbers are all anyone has to go on. A thief with your password can simply become you.

Choose your password wisely. Ideally, you want a password that is not really a word at all. Rather you should try for a mixture of upper- and lowercase letters as well as some numbers and even a symbol or two. You might also consider using a cryptic phrase combining upper- and lowercase letters that you can remember and that makes sense only to you, such as "keytothekingDOM."

Stay away from a single word that can be found in a dictionary. Thieves often use password-guessing software, and that's the first thing they look for. Just as obvious is your birthday, your address, your Social Security number, a common nickname, a family member's name, or your favorite color.

You should also change your password often, as a hacker is bound to get lucky sooner or later. And log-ins should be shut out for anyone who types in an unauthorized password three times in a row.

When you're sending other personal identification numbers over the Internet, such as your credit card number, make sure your number is being sent via encryption technology. Encryption scrambles the information so that only the proper eyes can see what you're sending. Most of the companies that do business on the Web provide for encryption. PC hardware and software sellers top the list. But even many of these cus-

tomers are still sufficiently scared of their credit card number being stolen that while they shop for their computer over the Net, they still make their purchases over the telephone.

Is that rational? Yes and no, but most of these risks are relative. If you choose to order over the phone, but then use a cordless or cell phone, that's not very safe, either. Anyone with a scanner can listen in on your conversation and pilfer your credit card number. It happens all the time. Encryption technology is not foolproof, but the harder it is for hackers to break a code, the more likely they are to move on to an easier target.

Finally, to feel extra safe, be sure to install a comprehensive data security package on your computer that includes simple encryption schemes, a virus protection utility, and an audit trail. You'll save money by purchasing these components as a package deal.

Shopping Safely on the Net

As more and more people wade out onto the Internet, businesses are emerging to handle both the new customers and their financial safety concerns. The Net is the ultimate shopping mall, with more choices than you could imagine. But customers still don't want to transmit their credit card number through cyberspace.

As a result of this fear, several firms are providing businesses and consumers with a "virtual cash" option that gives shoppers more security. These companies let you make Internet transactions without having to give out your credit card number after each purchase.

One such firm is First Virtual Holdings, Inc. Shoppers obtain a "VirtualPIN" number from First Virtual, which holds the customer's credit card information. Every time you shop, you use the VirtualPIN, not your credit card, to make purchases. Several thousand merchants currently accept the VirtualPIN as payment. Your transactions are then confirmed by e-mail before being posted to a credit card network over dedicated and secure phone lines, not the Internet.

Questions to Ask Before Doing Business Online

You need to put on your thinking cap before you make any major purchases online. After all, thousands of dollars can be changing hands without either party looking the other in the eye. So ask yourself a few questions before you click on your mouse.

- *"Do I know these people?"* You really should stick with companies that you've heard of. There's no sense saving a few dollars from a no-name Web site that might be out of business tomorrow. At the very least, make sure you can confirm the seller's physical address.

- *"Do they take security seriously?"* It makes sense to stick with companies that use encryption technology to secure your personal financial information. You can ask companies about their procedures pointblank via e-mail. You can also look at the bottom of the computer screen to see if there's a padlock icon. That icon indicates that the encryption mechanism is enabled.

- *"Will they give me the details of the deal in writing?"* Be sure to have the company e-mail you the specifics of the purchase, including a delivery date. Then contact them at once if they break their word.

The price for this peace of mind is $2 annually for the customer and a few hundred dollars for the participating businesses. You can get more information about First Virtual from their Web site (HYPERLINK http://www.firstvirtual.com).

Another company with a similar concept is CyberCash. You start the process by downloading an "electronic wallet." Here again you do give up your credit card number, but only once. CyberCash links up consumers, bank networks, and merchants so that every time you click on a purchase, your electronic wallet enables businesses to obtain bank authorization and issue electronic receipts. For purchases of less than $10, you can also use CyberCoin, which debits money from your checking account instead of your credit card.

There is no cost to consumers with CyberCash, although participating businesses have to chip in. Hundreds of merchants don't seem to mind and accept CyberCash and CyberCoin, including Macy's and Oracle. For more information, just click on the CyberCash Web site (HYPERLINK http://www.cybercash.com).

What to Do if You've Been Cyber-Swindled

No matter how many precautions you take to be safe when shopping on the Internet, you're bound to run into problems. Maybe your order is not shipped on time, or maybe it's not shipped at all. Or perhaps your credit card number falls into the hands of a thief who runs up a bunch of charges.

Luckily, many of the same laws that protect you when you shop in the real world will protect your Web purchases. Under the Fair Credit Billing Act, your liability for unauthorized credit card charges is limited to $50, as long as you report the incident within 60 days. The same liability for bank account debits falls under the Electronic Fraud Transfers Act.

You also have legal recourse if you make an Internet buy from a company that promises to send you the item within a specified period of time and then reneges on the deal. Under the law a company must ship you the item within the time stated in its ads. If no date is promised, the firm should send the item within 30 days after receiving your order or give you what is called an "option notice," which allows you to agree to the delay or cancel and get your money back.

For more information on federal and state laws dealing with consumer protection, you might want to go back to chapter 2, which explores the issue in more detail.

Tips to Be Safe on the Internet

Just keep in mind that once your computer is connected to the Internet it's not just a computer anymore. It's a gateway to millions of other computers all around the world. Most of the people behind those computers are as honest as you are. But a small minority are scam artists who will take your money unless you're careful.

Print a copy of your order forms and confirmation numbers for all your purchases and keep them for your records. The data in cyberspace might be easy to access, but it's the information that's on paper that you can use in court to get justice.

Closely review your monthly bank and credit card statements. If you start seeing charges that you didn't make, the sooner you respond the better. Remember, in the case of the Fair Credit Billing Act, you have a 60-day grace period.

Always be aware that any information you send over e-mail, whether it's your credit card number or a personal message, is not private (unless it's encrypted). Also, your work e-mail may be monitored by your employer. So think about that before you start e-mailing Viagra jokes to your cube mates.

WRAPPING *it* up

CHAPTER TEN

You can now see what your personal financial options are as you map out your own economic plan. But there's no guarantee that the current financial landscape will be the same 10 or 20 years from now.

It's important to look ahead to see some of the trends that may shape your financial future.

Key Things to Remember from This Book

Managing your personal finances is a serious matter, but it doesn't have to be mysterious. By taking lessons from this book you can assess your financial risks and needs, plan ahead, and save and invest to achieve your definition of financial success.

If you fall prey to scams or other types of fraud, you now know what laws you have on your side. You don't have to be a victim. Exercise your rights, get everything in

writing, and don't give up until you get satisfaction. When it comes to the investment world, you now know that the financial markets are not only for the affluent, they exist for you as well. You can invest in stocks, bonds, mutual funds, and other instruments according to your risk tolerance and investment philosophy.

Long-term financial planning, such as for college or retirement, should also now be easier to understand. You know you have to start preparing early, and that the primary responsibility is yours to make these goals a reality. Luckily, there are certain tax incentives (many of them brand new) and government programs to make things a little easier. Whether it's the new Roth IRA for retirement or the Lifetime Learning Credit for school, it pays to know what your constantly changing options are.

Insurance issues make up another part of your financial plan. No matter what your current health is, you now know that health insurance is a must, though what type you need is a personal choice that you'll decide based on cost and coverage factors. Homeowner's insurance and auto coverage are seemingly just as complicated to understand, but you should now have a better bird's-eye view of what's out there, what's required, and what the price may be. And when it comes to optional insurance, like disability insurance or umbrella policies, you should have a better understanding of why it might make sense to invest in these policies to protect you and your family.

Estate planning may force you to think about your own mortality, but you can now take some comfort in knowing that you do have some control over how your assets are disbursed to your loved ones, both while you're living and even decades after you pass away. And finally, recall risks you're vulnerable to when you shop online, and what precautions you can take to protect your privacy and your money.

Future Trends

Understanding the current economic landscape is important, but it's equally vital to stay abreast of possible new developments that could force you to alter your financial plan. So let's take a crystal-ball look at some of the issues you can anticipate in the decades to come—with the understanding that these projections may come with only varying degrees of accuracy.

For example, some forecasters in the 1960s predicted a wave of new gadgets, ranging from personal computers to cell phones, and speculated that new technology would allow us to work less and give us more free time than we could ever imagine. Well, as we now know, they got it half right. The past 30 years have indeed seen technological advances that are simply staggering. But despite all this new technology, we're still working as hard as before, maybe more so.

This trend will continue into the foreseeable future. For example, technology will make it more and more normal to work out of your home. That should be of some help to your family life and should allow you to work at your own pace. But new technology and new working environments will not diminish by one bit the workload that you're currently carrying. In fact, you'll be doing more important work because all the menial tasks that used to take up a chunk of your workday will now be taken care of.

Trends in the Economy

Financial reality is that the global economy will continue to intertwine us. You'll continue to see American-type cars being built in Japan and Japanese-type cars being built in America. The concept of a product being "made in the USA" will hold less and less meaning as people simply search for the best performance at the lowest price. This kind of competition will also make everyone work harder. A smaller economic world may open up more markets for our goods, but it also means there will be more competitors in our market.

Global interdependence also suggests that if Europe or even the farthest corner of Asia should start to languish economically, we will feel the effects. We've already seen this numerous times on Wall Street as hiccups in the Asian financial markets have sent the Dow and other important benchmarks into a free fall. This trend will continue, which is why it's more important than ever to be a patient investor and ride out the wild fluctuations that are sure to come.

Productivity should continue to rise. All the horror stories of downsizing and reengineering that received so much media play in the late 1980s and early 1990s have

given way to news about how productive corporate America has become. It may have come at a terrible cost, but today businesses are doing more with fewer employees, and they are constantly increasing their earnings. These growing earnings, combined with low inflation, have helped fuel the bull market.

And computer productivity should even outpace human productivity. A maxim known as Moore's Law states that computer productivity doubles every 18 months. With that in mind, it's easy to believe reports of all sorts of new uses for computer chips. By early next century, many financial experts predict that you'll be able to transact all your personal financial business using one "smart" card.

This card promises to be the ultimate credit card, replacing the money in your wallet, your ATM card, your health insurance card, your ID, and your other personal data. That kind of convenience and consolidation should save you time and money, but you'll have to keep your card in a safe place. Scam artists could have a field day with that kind of access to your money.

All of these technological and financial advances must be tempered by the specter of our becoming two societies, not based on gender or race, but rather divided by culture and access to technology. This development may affect the economy that you'll be working in.

When it comes to culture and class, the numbers are not optimistic. According to the Children's Defense Fund, one in four children are born poor, and one in seven have no health insurance. Further, one in three children are born to unmarried parents, and one in four are born to a mother who did not graduate from high school. These children represent a huge segment of the population, and they're starting out in life with a lot going against them.

As they grow up in the decades to come, many will be successful and add to the economic productivity that we looked at before. But others will be a drain on our economic and governmental resources. Just how much of a drain is hard to know, but this problem is one factor to consider when projecting our place in the world economy and our ability to compete. And access to technology, in schools, in libraries, at home, and at work, will be another key factor in how well we are able to compete.

Trends in Investing

Investing and the financial markets used to be a relatively secret realm, familiar to just a small segment of the population. This world was run by and for the mostly upper class, the mostly male, and the mostly white.

Today the average investor more resembles the average American. For example, the average mutual fund owner has a family income of around $50,000. Not bad, but certainly not a robber baron, either. Also, almost half of mutual fund owners are women. Mutual fund shareholders tend to be well educated, with a majority possessing at least a college degree, and most are long-term investors (they've been in the markets for at least ten years) with long-term needs.

These long-term goals, whether it's financing retirement, a home, or a child's college education, tend to make the average investor more patient and not subject to the hysteria that you sometimes see with the seasoned professional investing "experts." This is important to note because when the next bear market hits, it's the average, private, citizen-investor who will decide whether a market sell-off leads to long-term trouble or merely a good buying opportunity.

And don't fool yourself, bull markets don't last forever. Factors that contribute to a bear market include a jump in inflation, interest rates, or unemployment, a decline in corporate profits, and political instability either here or abroad. Any one of these factors could send stocks lower.

But it's not the one-day 500-point drop that you have to worry about. We've seen that before, and investors have simply laughed it off. Rather, what would happen if the Dow dropped the same 500 points, but did so a lot more slowly, say over the period of one or two years? The drop might technically be the same, but the reaction from investors would be quite different. Dollars tend to chase the highest return, and if that isn't in stocks then investors, patient or not, might begin to look at other vehicles for their money.

And that's when things could get ugly. Investors, who may have been slow to get out of stocks at the beginning of the bear market, might begin to lose confidence in equities. If that were to happen, it could take quite awhile for investors to regain that

confidence, even well after the point when it made sense to buy back into stocks.

All of this speculation is not meant to scare you. Rather, it's to emphasize that your financial plan should be based on reality and not the sugar-sweetened stock market returns of the past decade. Markets go up and markets go down, but as long as you're prepared to invest on a consistent, long-term basis, and your investments are within your risk tolerance as well as your means, you should be fine.

Another trend in investing deals with consolidation in the financial services industry. There's a move afoot to remove many of the regulations that govern how you buy mutual funds and insurance. Soon you'll be able to go to a bank, brokerage, or insurance company and have one-stop shopping for all your financial needs.

This consolidation won't happen tomorrow, but the groundwork is already in place. In the spring of 1998, for example, the House of Representatives passed a bill that would repeal large parts of the Glass-Steagall Act, a Depression era law that, along with subsequent regulations, created a firewall between what services banks, securities firms and insurance companies can provide. The law was originally passed to protect the financial services industry from intermingling its assets and risking a financial domino effect should the economy sour. Supporters of the legislation promise lower costs to consumers by increasing competitions, and added that customers will soon be able to track all their assets on one monthly statement. Opponents question how much competition will be fostered if the bill leads to an explosion of mergers and buyouts, which may lessen, not increase, consumer choice.

This debate is far from over, but it is likely you'll be seeing more consolidation and more of a willingness on the federal government's part to let business work things out on its own.

Trends in Government

Trying to predict the future actions, as well as the size, of the federal government is also important. As we saw in chapter 2, government plays quite a role in your per-

sonal finances, not just in the taxes you pay but in the regulations it imposes. Over the past 50 years the federal government's responsibilities have grown tremendously, as legislators have tried to set certain fundamental standards for all Americans: guaranteed retirement benefits, basic medical benefits, a minimum wage, clean air, and clean water, just to name a few.

But over the past five years the federal government has started to turn much of its responsibilities over to states and localities. We have also seen a deregulation of farming and telecommunications, as well as a welfare overhaul that removes Congress and the president from much of the decision making. The scope of the federal government is beginning to shrink, and that trend will continue.

But does that mean government will totally get out of the business of raising new taxes, creating new programs, and doling out special tax breaks? Well, let's do the math. In 1964 there were less than 17,000 registered lobbyists in Washington. Today there are more than 67,000—that's 125 lobbyists for each member of Congress. And many of these lobbyists are fighting for more money for their unique causes. So are the days of federal influence and congressional goodies over? What do you think?

The federal government will definitely play a role in the future, and still quite a large one, actually. But there can be no doubt that when it comes to regulations and incentives, the federal government will pick its fights and take only a limited incremental approach.

For example, look at the tax cuts that were passed with much fanfare in 1997. For all the hoopla and promises of more money in your pocket, the average tax cut for families making less than $59,000 was $6, which of course is better that a $6 tax hike. The point is, don't look to government to increase your wealth—you're on you own.

Keep Your Eye on the Baby Boomers

Another trend to watch out for involves the 76 million Americans born between 1946 and 1964, also known as the Baby Boomers. Well, they're not babies anymore;

many are now in their fifties. How the boomers fair leading up to their retirement days, and into their Golden Years will in large part dictate the shape of the economy in the early part of the next century. Plan accordingly.

A brief look at the history shows the power this generation wields. At every stage of their collective lives boomers have had an impact, both economic and social. In the 1950s and 1960s, they put severe pressure on the nation's school system; in the 1960s and 1970s, their adolescence contributed to a rise in crime; and into the 1970s and 1980s, boomers, looking to settle down and buy a home, affected the housing market and sent it skyward.

By the 1980s and especially into the 1990s, boomers started to realize that they weren't kids anymore and began to invest for retirement; that has helped send the stock market soaring. What's next? Well, look at what their needs will be in their sunset years and that should be an indication of where there will be increased demand.

Looking Ahead

In chapter 1 we saw several real-life examples of how people manage and mismanage their personal finances. Maybe you saw a little of yourself in some of the profiles. And just like you, these people have both near-term and long-term financial goals. Morgan and JeNell would like to start a family and have the funds to make their children's lives comfortable. Jennifer would like to be in more of a management role at work and also indulge her passion for travel. "I'd like to leave the country once a year," she says. Song would like the ultimate management role—to be her own boss. And Michael would like to make his fortune in the stock market, and along the way save for his retirement years.

Their goals might be different, but how they'll reach those objectives is surprisingly similar. And it's the same way you'll reach your goals. Write down what long-term goals you have, define what financial success means to you, and then map out how you will get there. Reading this book was a step in the right direction, but don't stop there. Make use of all the resources listed both in each chap-

ter and in the resources section at the end of the book. They are meant to provide you with answers to any questions you might have.

Then start investing, letting time be your greatest ally, and don't be rattled by every market hiccup. As you amass assets be sure you buy insurance for protection. Most of all, don't look for fairy godmothers to bail you out and secure your future—remember, you're on your own. But in a way, that's how it should be, because you're the only one who truly knows what you want.

GLOSSARY

aggressive growth stock: Stock in newer, smaller companies that have high growth potential.

Americans with Disabilities Act: A federal law that requires employers with 15 or more employees to make reasonable accommodations to individuals with disabilities.

annual percentage rate (APR): is the cost of credit, expressed as a yearly rate.

ATM card: A bank card that allows you to access your money from automatic teller machines around the world (for a small fee, of course).

auto insurance: Coverage that can include bodily injury liability, property damage liability, collision insurance, comprehensive insurance, medical payments coverage, and uninsured motorist's coverage.

bankruptcy: Legal process by which you liquidate your assets or restructure your debts to pay off your creditors.

bond: An interest-bearing debt instrument.

broker: An individual who makes financial transactions for you and may give investment advice.

coinsurance: The breakdown of how much you pay for a health care charge and how much your insurer pays.

Consolidated Omnibus Budget Reconciliation Act (COBRA): A federal law that requires employers with 20 or more employees to offer continued health coverage to employees who leave the firm and would otherwise be left uninsured.

credit report: A document that provides specific personal financial data, such as whether you pay your bills on time.

disability insurance: Insurance that supplements your income should an injury end or limit your ability to hold a job.

dollar-cost averaging: An investment strategy whereby an investor contributes equal amounts of money to an investment at regular intervals.

Education IRA: An investment option for college tuition that allows you to contribute $500 per year and pay no taxes as the money grows, as well as no taxes upon withdrawal.

Expected Family Contribution (EFC): The amount students and their families are expected to chip in for college costs before financial aid is given.

Employee Retirement Income Security Act (ERISA): A federal law passed in 1974 that sets certain minimum standards for pension plans.

Fair Credit Billing Act: A federal law that gives you legal recourse to fight billing errors on your credit card.

Fair Credit and Charge Discount Disclosure Act: A federal law that provides the right to compare all the terms and fees that various card issuers may offer.

Fair Credit Reporting Act: A federal law that gives you legal recourse if there are black marks on your credit report.

Family and Medical Leave Act: A federal law that allows you to take up to 12 weeks off from work to care for a sick family member or to take care of your own medical needs, without fear of being fired. The law applies only to firms with 50 or more employees.

401(k): An employer-sponsored retirement plan that allows you and your employer to set aside pretax dollars to fund your retirement account. The money grows tax-free until you make withdrawals.

Free Application for Federal Student Aid (FAFSA): A government document that you need to fill out for college aid. It asks you about your household and financial information and establishes your Expected Family Contribution. [See: Expected Family Contribution (EFC).]

global fund: A type of mutual fund that invests in all countries, including the United States.

grace period: The time between the date of a credit card purchase and the date interest starts being charged on that purchase.

growth funds: A type of mutual fund that buys into well-established medium-to-large firms that promise a slow but steady long-term march upward in price.

Health Insurance Portability and Accountability Act: A federal law that provides for continuous access to health insurance regardless of any health problems. The law also created Medical Savings Accounts (MSAs) that let you make tax-deductible contributions to the MSA. You then use the account to pay off your medical bills. Any money that you don't have to use in any given year gets to grow with the taxes deferred.

homeowner's insurance: Covers loss or damage of property, and personal liability.

HOPE Scholarship: A federal credit, available only for the first two years of college, that provides up to $1,500 per student for college tuition and fees.

indemnity health plans: Also called fee-for-service, this traditional health insurance gives you free choice over who you pick as your doctor, though you'll have to pay for a percentage of the bill. [See: coinsurance.]

index funds: A type of mutual fund that attempts to match a market benchmark, such as the Dow or the S&P 500, by buying all the stocks in that benchmark.

Individual Retirement Account (IRA): An account that lets you shelter up to $2,000 a year tax-free until you make withdrawals. Lower income taxpayers can also deduct their contributions from their taxes.

inflation: The rate at which the real cost of goods and services rise in the economy.

international funds: A type of mutual fund that invests two-thirds of the portfolio in securities of firms outside the United States.

Keogh: A self-employed retirement vehicle with tax incentives.

Lifetime Learning Credit: A federal tax credit of up to $1,000 to pay for college tuition and fees or graduate or professional school. The credit can only be used once on each tax return.

managed care health plan: These cost-containment plans include HMOs (Health Maintenance Organizations), PPOs (Preferred Provider Organizations), and POSs (Point of Service plans). They place different types of restrictions on which doctors you can see, and in return they pay for a larger part of your medical bills than traditional indemnity.

marriage penalty: A quirk in the tax law that causes higher income couples with roughly the same income to pay more in taxes than if they filed as single. The opposite effect is the "marriage bonus," which causes mostly lower income couples to pay less in taxes than if they filed as single.

mutual fund: An investment vehicle that pools the money of hundreds or thousands of investors to allow them to buy into stocks, bonds, and other investments.

Pension Benefit Guaranty Corporation (PBGC): The organization charged with insuring most defined-benefit pensions.

permanent insurance: A class of life insurance that offers more flexibility than term policies. Permanent plans may also include a feature known as "cash value," which gives you the choice to cancel your policy during your lifetime and get the cash value of the plan in a lump sum.

prepaid college tuition plans: A relatively new concept that allows you to pay for future university tuition costs in today's dollars.

price-to-earnings ratio: A measure of a stock's value, calculated by dividing the stock's current share price by its earnings per share.

probate: The legal and public procedure that governs how your estate is distributed.

pyramid scams: Illegal schemes that promise sizable future dollars if you put in a little money up front. Early participants get paid with the contributions of later applicants. Eventually, the pyramid collapses due to an ever-growing need for participants.

Roth IRA: A new type of IRA that allows you to make tax-free withdrawals as well as enjoy tax-free growth. The catch is that the money you contribute can't be deducted from your taxes.

slamming: The switching of your long-distance carrier without your permission.

spam: Junk mail that invades your computer.

stock: A share of ownership in a corporation.

telemarketers: People who sell goods or services over the phone. Telemarketing can be legal or illegal depending on pressure techniques or misrepresentations.

temps: Temporary employees who generally do not receive health insurance or have contributions put into their company's retirement plan.

term insurance: A type of life insurance policy that gives you protection for a specified period of time, and if you die during that time the policy pays out a benefit.

trust: A legal arrangement that enables an individual, called a grantor, to hold property for another person or a group of other people. The assets fall under the control of a trustee, who manages and distributes the assets according to the wishes of the grantor.

umbrella policies: Insurance protection that is designed to give you maximum coverage and extend past your other insurance.

U.S. Government bond fund: A type of mutual fund that buys securities from the U.S. Treasury and debt issued by federal agencies.

will: A legal document that dictates your financial and personal wishes after you're gone.

Y2K problem: Potential upcoming financial crisis dealing with computer systems. Computers that read years as two digits (1998 as "98," for example) will be confused by the year 2000 and may misinterpret transactions made in the year 2000 as being made in the year 1900.

RESOURCES

Books and Reports

The Beardstown Ladies' Common-Sense Investment Guide. The Beardstown Ladies' Investment Club with Leslie Whitaker (Hyperion, 1994).

College Financial Aid for Dummies. Dr. Herm Davis and Joyce Lain Kennedy (IDG Books, 1997).

The Complete Book of Insurance: The Consumer's Guide to Insuring Your Life, Health, Property and Income. Ben G. Baldwin (Probus, 1996).

Get Rich Slow. Tama McAleese (Career Press, 1995).

Invest Your Way to Wealth. Theodore Miller (Times Business, 1996).

Investment Biker. Jim Rogers (Adams Publishing, 1994).

The Value Line Investment Survey, P.O. Box 3988, New York, NY 10008, (800) 833-0046, $570/yr., weekly.

Magazines

Kiplinger's Personal Finance. 3401 East-West Highway, Hyattsville, MD 20782, (800) 544-0155, $19.95/yr., monthly.

Money. P.O. Box 60001, Tampa, FL 33660, $39.95/yr., 13 issues. *Smart Money.* P.O. Box 7538, Red Oak, IA 51591, (800) 444-4204, $24/yr., monthly.

Consumer Groups

To sort out your debt problems: Consumer Credit Counseling Service (CCCS), (800) 388-2227.

Consumer Federation of America. 1424 16th St., NW, Washington, DC 20036, (202) 387-6121.

Health Insurance Association of America. 555 13th St., NW, Suite 500, Washington, DC 20036, (202) 778-3200.

To get information on privacy issues: Privacy Rights Clearinghouse, at 1717 Kettner Ave., Suite 105, San Diego, CA 92101, (619) 298-3396.

Credit Reporting Services

Equifax, P.O. Box 740241, Atlanta, GA 30374-0241, (800) 685-1111.

Experian, P.O. Box 949, Allen, TX 75013; (800) 682-7654.

Trans Union, 760 West Sproul Rd., P.O. Box 309, Springfield, PA 19064-0390, (800) 916-8800

Government Resources

For "slamming" complaints: Federal Communications Commission, Common Carrier Bureau, Enforcement Division, Informal Complaints and Public Inquires Branch, Mail Stop Code 1600A2, 2025 M St., NW, Washington, DC 20554.

For Fair Credit Billing Act enforcement issues: Federal Trade Commission, Correspondence Branch, Washington, DC 20580.

For information from the body that administers and regulates private pensions: The U.S. Labor Department's Pension and Welfare Benefits Administration, 200 Constitution Ave., NW, Washington, DC 20210. For brochures: (800) 998-7542.

For postal fraud: Chief Postal Inspector, United States Postal Service, Washington, DC 20260, (202) 268-4267.

For an estimate of how your Social Security payments are growing: Social Security Administration, (800) 772-1213; ask for a free Personal Earnings and Benefits Estimate Statement.

For stocks fraud: Securities and Exchange Commission, 450 5th St., NW, Washington, DC 20006, (202) 728-8233

Other Useful Organizations

Certified Financial Planner Board of Standards, 1660 Lincoln St., Suite 3050, Denver, CO 80264-3001, (800) CFP-MARK.

Chartered Financial Consultants, The American College, 270 Bryn Mawr Ave., Bryn Mawr, PA, 19010 (215) 526-1000.

National Association of Securities Dealers, 1735 K St., NW, Washington, DC 20006, (202) 728-8044.

National Committee for Quality Assurance, which accredits HMOs and other managed care organizations, 2000 L Street, NW, Suite 500, Washington, DC 20036, (800) 839-6487.

Online Resources

American College of Trust and Estate Counsel's estate planning site, HYPERLINK http://www.actec.org

American Medical Association's doctor information site, HYPERLINK http://www.ama-assn.org

Bank Rate Monitor's credit card information, HYPERLINK http://www.bankrate.com

Better Business Bureau, HYPERLINK http://www.bbb.com

The College Board financial aid information site, HYPERLINK http://www.collegeboard.org

Federal Emergency Management Agency's disaster relief information site, HYPER-LINK http://www.fema.gov

Federal Trade Commission, HYPERLINK http://www.ftc.gov

Firms that rate the financial strength of companies: A.M. Best, HYPERLINK http://www.ambest.com and Weiss Ratings, HYPERLINK http://www.weissratings.com

Insurance Information Institute's Web page, HYPERLINK http://www.iii.org

Investment Company Institute's investment information, HYPERLINK http://www.ici.org

IRS tax information and advice, HYPERLINK http://www.irs.ustreas.gov

Junk Busters site that helps you fight spammers, HYPERLINK http://www.junk-busters.com, www.junkbusters.com

Quackwatch's health fraud site, HYPERLINK http://www.quackwatch.com

The Scholarship Page, for all types of college scholarships, HYPERLINK http://www.iwc.pair.com/scholarshipage

Securities and Exchange Commission's EDGAR financial database, HYPERLINK http://www.sec.gov

Stock exchange Web sites: The American Stock Exchange, HYPERLINK http://www.amex.com, The New York Stock Exchange, HYPERLINK http://www.nyse.com, and Nasdaq HYPERLINK http://www.nasdaq.com

Telecommunications Research and Action Center, HYPERLINK http://www.trac.com

Term insurance quote services: QuickQuote, HYPERLINK http://www.quick-quote.com, and Quotesmith, HYPERLINK http://www.quotesmith.com

U.S. Consumer Gateway site for advice on your health, your home, your money, and product safety, HYPERLINK http://www.consumer.gov

U.S. Department of Education's college financial aid site, HYPERLINK http://www.ed.gov/offices/ope/

INDEX